Hydro-Electricity in North West Wales

Dewi W Thomas

ISBN: 0-86381-455-7

Printed by Gwasg Carreg Gwalch,
12 Iard yr Orsaf, Llanrwst, Wales LL26 0EH.
☎ (01492) 642031

Cover photo:
Cwm Dyli power station looking across the valley with the access track and main road on the left

CONTENTS

LIST OF FIGURES

LIST OF PHOTOGRAPHS

LIST OF PHOTOGRAPHS - continued

ACKNOWLEDGEMENTS

My sincere thanks and appreciation for assistance in varying forms are due to the following:

Richard Edwards, Llanuwchllyn
Steffan ap Owain, Gwynedd Archives Service, Dolgellau
Staff at the Public Records Office, Kew
Arthur C Thomas and Brian Woolaway, Llechwedd Quarry
Liz Spengler, Museum of Science and Industry, Manchester
Morgan Williams, Trefriw Woolen Mills
Bill Jones, Blaenau Ffestiniog (Fforwm Plas Tanybwlch)
Goronwy Howells, Maentwrog Power Station
Fred Cook and Alun Jones, Dwr Cymru
John Baxendale, National Power Hydro, Dolgarrog
Jeffrey T Davies, Rhyl

Also I am indebted to Lesley Baxendale for her skills and inventiveness relating to word processing.

Hydro-Electricity in North West Wales

Chapter 1

INTRODUCTION

North West Wales is an area of outstanding natural beauty which includes the Snowdonia National Park, and for the purposes of this study, coincides approximately with the present county of Gwynedd. The ancient kingdom of Gwynedd covered almost the same land area. Gwynedd as it now is, was formed from the previous counties of Anglesey, Caernarfon and Merioneth in 1974. These old counties are scheduled to re-appear under different titles because of Local Government Reorganisation.

This part of Wales is dominated by the rugged mountains of Snowdonia and the long coastlines of Conwy Bay, Caernarfon Bay and the Cambrian coast.
The total population of the area was only 101,300 in 1801, increasing by 110% to 212,720 by 1901; rising marginally to 213,155 in 1971[1] and remaining fairly constant thereafter apart from influxes at peak holiday times. The bulk of the population was and still is concentrated on the coastal regions. The more rugged and barren areas have remained largely unchanged for centuries.

Early industrial activity was confined to fulling mills and flour mills utilising water power. Hone quarries were to be found in the inaccessible mountainous regions whilst slate mines and quarries expanded from small almost single-handed ventures into a major industry exporting quality slate to many foreign countries.

Breweries were located close to many towns and tanneries produced leather for wearing apparel and agricultural purposes. Paper mills also water powered could also be found. One was sited on the River Seiont near Caernarfon whilst another utilised water from the River Porthllwyd in the Conwy valley.

Other mining activities extracted lead, copper and gold.

The consolidation and expansion of the slate producing industry brought about a concerted expansion in the shipbuilding trade. Early vessels were constructed at many points with access to the open sea, on beaches, or sheltered coves. Ships of various tonnages were constructed at Amlwch, Nefyn, Conwy, Caernarfon, Pwllheli, Barmouth and Aberdovey. A late entrant was Portmadoc which did not exist as a town prior to 1820 and the raising of the embankment across the River Glaslyn a few years previously. From 1826 to 1860 a total of 136 vessels were built at Portmadoc and from 1860 onwards the numbers varied between 3 and 5 vessels per year until 1913 when the final vessel the Gestiana was launched[2].

Closely associated with the shipbuilding industry were the timber yards and mills which utilised timber imported from North America. These mills were steam powered. Other users of steam power were the foundries that produced engineering items for agricultural, quarrying and shipping usage.

During the period of industrial growth the main activity within the area was still agriculture and farming, the bulk of the population being employed within this sphere. The railways laid down by the Chester and Holyhead Railway (later the LNWR) and the Cambrian Railways improved access and communications for the coastal regions especially. Several coastal towns expanded rapidly and became centres of concentrated population.

As previously mentioned, water was the source of power for industrial use in the smallest flour mills and also the largest slate quarries. Water wheels were to be seen in many places across the area and the millwrights were important tradesmen in any community. The first alternative source of power was gas produced in local small gas works originally by burning coal. Caernarfon had its first undertaking in 1833 and others followed at Pwllheli, Bala, Blaenau Ffestiniog, Holyhead, Corwen and Porthmadog. Barmouth had the largest gas producing plant in the old Merionethshire, producing 17,000 cubic feet of gas per annum.

These works could produce sufficient gas for local domestic demand but could not cope with industrial development or indeed on occasion, the increased demand from expanding townships.

The next alternative source of power nationally was to be electricity. In 1831 the discovery of electromagnetic induction by Michael Faraday was announced, precluding the possibility of converting mechanical power into electricity.

Shortly after Faraday's discovery, small generators became available, but it was not until 1857 that they were used to produce light in lighthouses. The electric arc light formed by an arc between two carbon rods gave a bright light and were used for lighting in public places. This form of lighting however was not suitable for domestic use. The situation changed when in 1878, Joseph Swan demonstrated that a carbon filament in an evacuated glass bulb would glow when an electric current was passed through it.

In December 1880, Sir William Armstrong installed Swan lamps in his house at Cragside, Northumberland, powering them from a water driven generator. In Britain the pioneer central electricity station was at Godalming in Surrey, where the German company Siemens installed and operated a water powered station in 1881 to light the streets and supply private consumers.

The Electricity Lighting Acts of 1882 and 1888 gave local authorities opportunities to develop electricity undertakings but many were unwilling to create competition for their own lucrative municipal gas undertakings. Another important consideration was the lack of technical knowledge and commercial uncertainty of this new and relatively untried form of power.

By the early 1890's small developments had occurred, confined mainly to reciprocating steam engine driven plants supplying a limited number of lamps within a small distance radius. Most of the early installations used direct current distributed over a wide area at large expense due to heavy transmission losses. The development of alternating current which could be transformed to higher voltages for more efficient transmission over longer distances opened up the possibilities of wider distribution areas.

These new advances and developments did not encroach upon North West Wales. The first hydro-electric power station for public supply in the North of England was established at Keswick in 1890. The earliest hydro-electric development of any magnitude was initiated in 1894 for the production of aluminium which for economic reasons required the continuous supply of low cost power. This first major hydro-electric scheme was the Foyers project situated on the eastern side of Loch Ness in Scotland, built by the British Aluminium Company Limited, and was completed in 1896. Even in those early days of hydro-electric development, opposition was active and the Foyers scheme was attacked on the question of amenities and the risk of fumes destroying trees. The total installed capacity of the plant was equivalent to 5000 horsepower and the plant produced about 200 tons of aluminium per annum in the early years of its existence.

Local authorities in North West Wales came to realise in the space of a few years that there was a market for electricity alongside the existing gas schemes. The first example of electricity being made available for domestic purposes was the system provided by Llandudno Town Council which commenced in 1895. This was followed by Bangor Corporation in 1897 and Caernarfon in 1902.

Several other local authorities commenced supplying electricity in succeeding years utilising steam power, the steam being produced in boilers fuelled with domestic or industrial refuse and coal.

Hydro electricity schemes however, were to become a major influence on the industrial scene in the area, especially concerning the slate producing quarries and mines. Power was required on an extensive scale for haulage purposes and the mines especially experienced continuous problems with water ingress into workings deep underground necessitating continuous pumping. Schemes purely for domestic purposes were concurrently developed. The basic requirements for any successful hydro-electric scheme were available in the form of high annual rainfall coupled with large storage at high level. Snowdonia had and still has amongst the highest annual rainfall amounts in Britain.

Chapter 2

HYDRO-ELECTRIC PIONEERS

In the formative years of hydro-electric development in North West Wales, three individuals in particular stand out as pioneering personalities. These three were Richard Edwards, T.P. Osborne Yale and Moses Kellow. Their background and upbringing contrasted greatly from one to the other and their contributions were also markedly different.

RICHARD EDWARDS (1861-1941)

Richard Edwards was born in 1861 in the parish of Llanuwchllyn, an agricultural community in the heart of the old county of Merionethshire close to where the rivers Dyfrdwy and Twrch combine before discharging into Llyn Tegid (Bala Lake). He was the son of Evan Edwards a farmer/joiner and his wife Mary.

The 1871 Census (RG10/5685)[3] gives the following information relating to the farm "Drwsynant Ucha"

Name	Relation to Head	Condition in Marriage	Age	Occupation	Where Born
Evan Edwards	Head	Married	62	Farmer/Joiner	Llanuwchllyn
Mary Edwards	Wife	Married	52	Farmers Wife	Dolgelley
John Edwards	Son	Single	26	Millwright	Llanuwchllyn
Evan Edwards	Son		16	Farmers Son	Llanuwchllyn
Cadwallader Edwards	Son		14	Farmers Son	Llanuwchllyn
Mary Edwards	Daughter		12	Scholar	Llanuwchllyn
Richard Edwards	Son		9	Scholar	Llanuwchllyn
Edward Edwards	Son		7	Scholar	Llanuwchllyn
Catherine Jones	Daughter	Married	18	Farmers Dghtr.	Llanuwchllyn
Mary A Jones	Gr.Daughter		3mth		Llanuwchllyn

From the above it can be seen that Evan Edwards a joiner, and his son John a millwright, were actively engaged in mill construction which included the manufacture of mill wheels. Richard is noted as a 9 year old scholar. What the bare facts do not reveal is that Richard was seriously injured at the age of 4 when he fell under a horse drawn sledge sustaining severe damage to his legs. As a consequence he was bed-ridden for a substantial period of time and was unable to partake in formal education. Whilst bed-ridden he learnt to read and developed a great interest in technical matters and inventions of the day. Richard later recovered well enough to assist on the farm and by 1891 as shown on the Census (RG12/4639)[4], again for Drwsynant, his occupation was that of a millwright.

Name	Relation to Head	Condition in Marriage	Age	Occupation	Where Born
Mary Edwards	Head	Widow	71	Farmer	Dolgelley
Ellen Edwards	Daughter	Single	40	Dressmaker	Llanuwchllyn
Cadwallader Edwards	Son	Single	34	Farmer	Llanuwchllyn
Richard Edwards	Son	Single	29	Millwright	Llanuwchllyn
Ellen	Gr.Daughter	Single	11		Llanuwchllyn

The year 1895 was very eventful for Richard because he became a married man and also rented the buildings associated with a tannery in the village of Llanuwchllyn where he established a millwright's workshop. These workshops were to employ up to 14 people in the manufacture of turbines to provide mechanical power for farm machinery. Motive power for the workshops originated from a waterwheel provided with water from the nearby River Twrch. Two houses were also constructed on the site to accommodate the family.

For the manufacture of the turbines, castings were purchased from the Britannia Foundry at Portmadoc. The construction of frames, all lathe-work, including bearing production together with initial assembly, was undertaken in Richard Edwards' workshop.

Turbines of various sizes were manufactured in Llanuwchllyn and installed throughout North and Mid Wales.

In 1909 the then Llanuwchllyn Parish Council approached Richard Edwards with a request for a scheme to install public lighting in the village utilising oil lamps. Mr Edwards suggested to the Parish Council that electric lighting would be more efficient and economical, there would be no need to employ a lamp-man whose duties would include lighting and extinguishing each individual lamp. The proposed scheme was accepted, poles were erected and wires strung not only for street lighting but also for house lighting. A 110 Volt DC dynamo was installed in the Edwards' workshop driven from the existing waterwheel and the supply commenced on 1st January 1910.

Less than a decade later, the number of houses in the village had increased considerably, all requiring the benefit of electric lighting and as a result, the demand was greater than the waterwheel driven dynamo could cope with. Richard Edwards therefore proceeded with an expansion programme to construct a small power house on the River Twrch. A weir was constructed across the river to divert water into a leat 3/4 of a mile in length which terminated in a 22 inch diameter pipeline above the purpose built building sited adjacent to the Pont-y-Pandy road bridge. It took 3 men a whole year to excavate 500 yards of the leat. The operating head available was 75 feet and the Pelton wheel turbine was a twin jet type with 2 inch and 4 inch nozzles revolving at 160 rpm. The dynamo was rated at 230 Volts DC; 1000 rpm. The power house came into operation in 1920.

As the domestic loading continued to increase it was later found necessary to supplement the system with diesel engine driven generators, the first to be installed being a Petter single cylinder diesel engine with a 3 ton flywheel.

The power house installed capacity of 25 Kw remained sufficient for many years. It was not until 1963 that the village supply was taken over by Manweb, supplying a total of 120 houses.

The following table[5] gives the particulars of the installations put down between 1907 and 1917 and gives the sizes of the installations together with the nature of the work for which the power was used.

(These statistics extracted from a paper entitled "Small Water Powers in North Wales" by Thomas Smith, a former Electrical Engineer to the Wolverhampton Corporation, dated 1918 and found in Enclosure A53581c of Power 2/28 classification at P.R.O.)

Number of Installations	Max. H.P.	Min. H.P.	Average H.P.	Total H.P.	Nature of work for which power is used
221	9	1	3.72	822	Farm power
13	7	2	3.50	45.5	Farm lighting
10	14	6	10.00	100	Corn mills
8	9	1	3.75	30	Pumping
6	16	7	11.20	67	Saw mills
4	27	5	14.00	56	Public supply
4	18	11	14.00	56	Quarries
2	2	2	2.00	4	Private houses lighting
1	13	-	-	13	Bakery
1	12	-	-	12	Clover mill
1	8	-	-	8	Tannery
1	5	-	-	5	Woollen factory
1	2	-	-	2	Laundry

The locations where turbines were installed by the Edwards family are shown in the map (*Figure 1*) given on the following page.

Figure 1 - The map shows locations where turbines of Richard Edwards' manufacture were installed, a remarkable proliferation to emanate from the workshop in Llanuwchllyn.

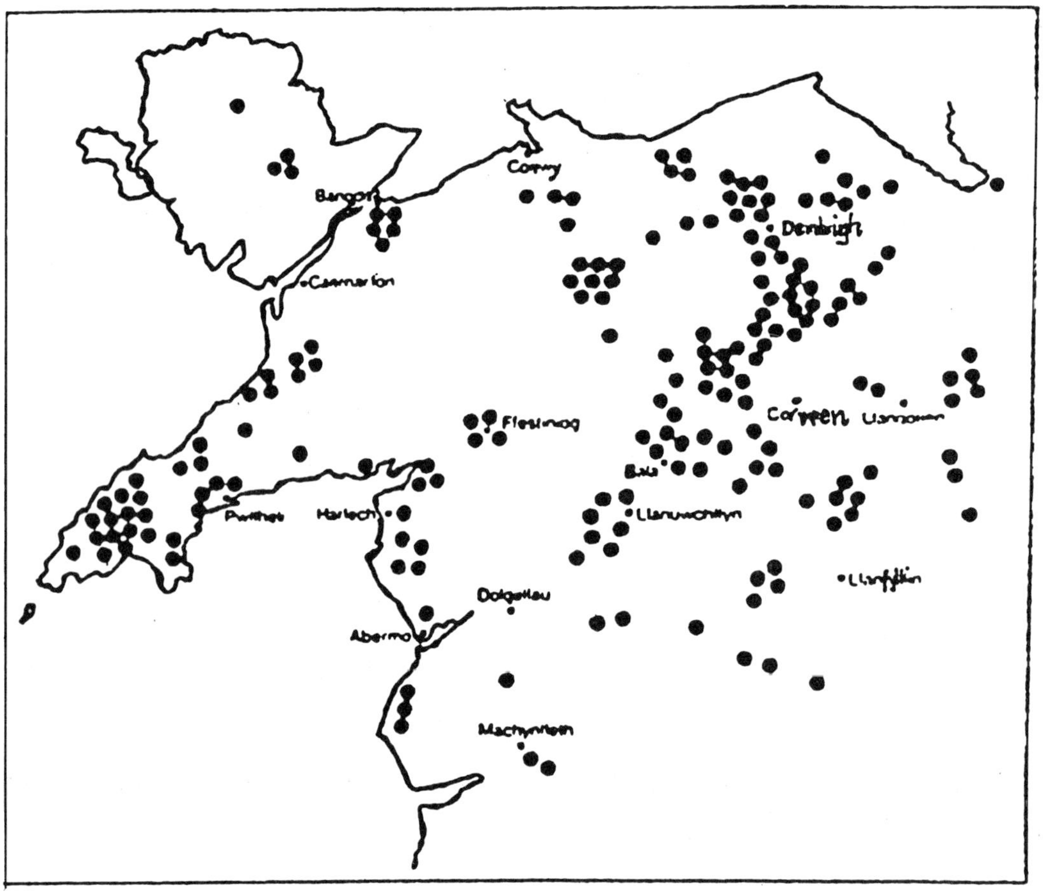

Richard Edwards was succeeded by his son, Antur Edwards and later his grandson, the present Richard Edwards. The Edwards family continue to reside in the properties erected in 1895 and a fitting tribute to Richard Edwards foresight and the skills of his employees is the fact that the power house remains operational, generating DC power for the domestic uses of the two houses. Generation takes place every day throughout the year with 8kW output during minimum water flow conditions. The only item of plant to be replaced has been the dynamo.

The following items of correspondence (*Figures 2 - 5*) provide an insight into the nature of business carried out by Richard Edwards, a remarkable person in many ways:

Figure 2:

COPY

ENCLOSURE No. 935

From/

Richard Edwards,
Millwright & Electric Engineer,
Llanuwchllyn, N.Wales.

To/

Mr. Colley,
The Aluminium Corporation,Ltd.,
Dolgarrog.

Dated 23rd August, 1923.

Dear Sir,

TALYBRAICH AND TALYWAEN.

I have pleasure in making the following report on the water power at the above farms from observations taken yesterday.

At Talybraich there is a 1½ H.P. Waterwheel in fairly good condition, working a churn and grindstone. This wheel is hardly powerful enough for driving a chaffcutter. It is a capital place for a pelton wheel where a fall of about 45 feet may be had in 76 yards of piping, consequently the same amount of power may be had from about one-sixth the volume of water.

I ascertained from the farmer that during a spell of dry weather about three months ago, there was just enough water to turn the wheel idle (but not to churn) and at the same time no water was running out of the Company's leet in the brook, nor was any water in the leat above the house.

From this, I gather there must be a supply coming into their brook lower down than the leat, if so, this supply alone if gathered into a pond may be quite sufficient to do all their work. The above reasons along are sufficient for not recommending the alaying of a pipe from the leat above the house.

The waterwheel put will serve as a pit for pelton wheel, and I am quoting for a 2 H.P. one fitted with a 1 H.P. nozzle the larger nozzle can be readily fitted if at any time the tenant requires it for chaff cutting.

TALYWAEN.

Here there is an old and very imperfect impulse wheel,

Fig. 2 cont...

quite out of order and had been so apparently for some time.

There is a fall of 24 ft. in 30 yards where a small tank used to be. This cannot be enlarged sufficient to work when the water supply is very low. I would recommend going some 30 yards further up where a fall of over 30 feet may be had, and where there is a room for a pond of sufficient capacity to run the wheel for an hour or so without depending on the incoming flow. This pond should be of about 30 cubic yards capacity say 10 yards x 9' x 3' or equal; both farms about the same. Ponds may be wholly made by excavation, therefore labour only is required. This labour together with cutting and closing pipe track is not included in the estimates.

Yours faithfully,

(sgd) R.Edwards.

Figure 3:

Quotations subject to change without notice.

All agreements are contingent upon strikes, accidents, and other delays beyond our control.

Aluminium Corporation Limited.

ALL COMMUNICATIONS TO BE ADDRESSED TO THE CORPORATION.

All goods to
DOLGARROG SIDINGS
near Llanrwst
L. & N. W. RLY.
unless otherwise instructed on order.

Telegrams.
FLUXODE, DOLGARROG.
Telephone.
20 TYN-Y-GROES (Llandudno)

Registered Office.
WELLINGTON HOUSE,
BUCKINGHAM GATE, S.W.1.
Telegrams. Fluxode, Sowest, London
Telephones. Victoria 9055 & 9056

MINES:- SILLANS-VAR.
Telegrams. Fluxode, Sillans-Var.
Code.
A.B.C. Fifth Edition.

YOUR REFERENCE

OUR REFERENCE
WHICH KINDLY GIVE IN YOUR REPLY.
CC/TB.

Head Offices:-
Clark Street.
Dolgarrog, 27th August 1923
NORTH WALES.

NATIONAL SCHEME FOR DISABLED MEN

H.J.Jack,Esq.,

LONDON OFFICE.

Dear Sir,

FARMS BELOW LLUGWY LAKE.

Herewith I beg to hand you copy of report with estimates from Mr.Edwards, the Water Turbine man whom we had over to inspect and report on the water supply to the above farms. He seems very reasonable in his charges, and the whole scheme as he suggests doing it is very much cheaper than any other scheme we have had put before us.

I have sent a copy of this report to Messrs.Fox for their observations, and unless they see some objection to Mr.Edwards' proposals, I suggest the best way would be to approach Mr.Trench for permission to make the ponds he suggests and lay the pipe lines.

Yours faithfully,
For the ALUMINIUM CORPORATION LIMITED.

C. Colley

CONSTRUCTION MANAGER.

Figure 4:

From/
Richard Edwards,
Millwright & Electric Engineer,
Llanuwchllyn, N.Wales.

To/
The Aluminium Corporation,
Dolgarrog.

Dated 23rd August, 1923.

TALYBRAICH.

I shall be pleased to undertake to supply anf fix a 2 H.P. Pelton wheel for churning and running a grindstone at Talybraich as under :-

One 44" x 6" Pelton Wheel on steel spindle running in brass bearings on iron frame, adapted for bolting on concrete work.

One 4" Screwdown valve with brass faces and gunmetal spindle worked by a handle and spindle from inside the dairy.

Pair of Cogwheels and connections to churn and a pulley on the outside also a pulley on grindstone spindle and with belt.

Sheey iron cover and a grating on entrance into pipe. Size of nozzle 1". Sizeefor 2 H.P. - 1.7/8" (not fitted at present).

Price, carriage paid Bettws-y-Coed and fixed £24.10.0.

The following pipes will be required :-

76 yards of 6" castiron socket. Present price coated and laid down and joined 14/6 per yard. Labour not included.

Yours truly,

(sgd) R.Edwards.

Figure 5:

<u>COPY.</u>

From/

Richard Edwards

Millwright & Electric Engineer,

Llanuwchllyn, N.Wales.

To/

The Aluminium Corporation Ltd.,
Dolgarrog.

<u>Dated 23rd August, 1923.</u>

<u>TALYWAEN.</u>

<u>Pelton wheel</u>, same description, as for Talybraich, but with 5" valve and a 1½" nossle and bare outside end for spindle. Price fixed £24 - or £46 for the two if ordered same time, covering previous expenses.

The following pipes will be required at Talywaen.

60 yards of 7" castiron socket. Present price delivered Bettws-y-Coed and laid - 15/9 per yard.

Yours truly,

(sgd) R.Edwards.

The above estimate does not include cement for the work. of which about 2 cwts. will be required with each, as the Corporation may be in a better position to supply this.

Yours etc.
R.Edwards.

TP OSBORNE YALE (1868 - 1922)

Thomas Parry Osborne Yale was a member of the ancient Yale family of Plâs-yn-Iâl (Yale Hall) Llandegla, Denbighshire, being the second surviving son of William Corbet Yale-Jones-Parry B.A. J.P.. Thomas was the first Yale to be born at Plâs-yn-Iâl for over 100 years.

Thomas' father William had inherited Madryn Castle in Lleyn and assumed the name Jones-Parry. Thomas came into two estates grossly in debt and mortgaged to the hilt, and therefore had neither the capital nor the time to carry out the many plans he had made for the restoration of Plâs-yn-Iâl. His tenure of the old family home lasted for only 12 years and he then resided with his family at Ty Gwyn, close to the Waterloo Bridge at Betws-y-Coed.

TP Osborne Yale became a qualified electrical engineer and under Articles of Association dated 27th January 1899, the Yale Electric Power Company Limited was formed for the purpose of developing the large amount of water power running to waste in the district of Blaenau Ffestiniog. Land was leased on the banks of the River Goedol for a power station site with the aim of supplying electricity to the slate mines and quarries in the area, together with electric lighting for the streets and private consumers. The whole scheme was carried out under the supervision of Thomas Yale, the managing director of the company.

A full account of the scheme is given in later chapters, however, at this point it can be noted that the company gave a 24 hour supply providing power to the slate mines and quarries for hauling, pumping and mill driving. The company also entered into an agreement with the Urban District Council to supply electricity for public and private lighting for a period of 15 years. This is believed to be the first time that a public electricity supply had been produced by water power in Great Britain and on 22nd May 1902, Lord Newborough performed the ceremony of inaugurating the public supply.

The Queens Hotel in Blaenau Ffestiniog was the first private property to be connected to the new supply followed by Brymer's Grocery store.

The initial minute book of the Yale Power Co.[6] is lodged at the Gwynedd Archives Dolgellau office (document reference Z/DAG/647). The first board meeting of the company was held at 1 & 2 Great Winchester Street, London on 22nd February 1899, at which were present, in addition to TPO Yale, the following: Major General H Percival; Messrs CE Green, FS Percival and JS Hughes, consulting engineer to the Votty and Bowydd Slate Quarries Co. Ltd. The date on incorporation was noted as being 31st January 1899 and the certificate of incorporation was numbered 60493. FS Percival was elected chairman, whilst JH Brady the secretary of the Votty and Bowydd company was appointed secretary with a salary of ten pounds per annum. The first ordinary general meeting of shareholders took place at the same venue on 5th May 1899.

TPO Yale guided the company through an extremely successful early period, but by 1918 his health was deteriorating and his letter of resignation was read at a board meeting of 12th August 1918.

Probate records show that Thomas Parry Osborne Yale of Ty Gwyn, Capel Garmon, Denbighshire died on 30th December 1922. Probate was granted in London on 29th May 1923.

MOSES KELLOW J.P.: M.Inst C.E.: M.I.Mech.E: M.I.Q: FGS (1862 - 1943)

Moses Kellow was born on 5th June 1862 at Old Delabole, Cornwall being the son of William and Charity Kellow. William Kellow was employed at the large slate quarry in Old Delabole, a few miles south of Tintagel. In 1865 the family moved to North Wales and resided in Caernarfon and later moved again to Tremadoc.

The 1871 Census (RG10/5700)[7] shows the family residing in Dublin Street, Tremadoc which was in the parish of Ynyscynhaiarn, as given below:

Name	Relation to Head	Condition in Marriage	Age	Occupation	Where Born
William Kellow	Head	Married	38	Foreman of Slate quarry	Tintagel, Cornwall
Charity Kellow	Wife	Married	32	-	Tintagel, Cornwall
Moses Kellow	Son		8	Scholar	St Treath, Cornwall
Mary A Kellow	Daughter		5	Scholar	Ynyscynhaiarn
Elizabeth Kellow	Daughter		2	-	Ynyscynhaiarn

Moses received his early training in engineering and geology from his father and before being 21 years old he was appointed manager of the Park Quarry at Croesor.

In January 1892, Moses married Nell the daughter of Thomas and Elizabeth Williams of Bryn, Croesor. Thomas Williams had been manager of the Croesor Quarry for many years and when he died in 1895, Moses Kellow took over the management of this quarry in addition.

Most of the following information has been extracted from the autobiography of Moses Kellow which is to be found in the Bangor University Library as Bangor MSS 5276.

In 1901 Moses Kellow prepared a scheme for the electrification of the Croesor quarry proposing to derive the power from the Cwm Foel valley which was 1460 feet above sea level. By constructing a dam in this valley together with laying a pipeline and building a generating station at the foot of the Croesor valley, he was able to utilise a head of 860 feet. A full specification for 3 phase generating plant was drawn up in 1902 and Moses travelled extensively in Europe visiting most of the works of the electrical manufacturers.

The original plant for the generating station was manufactured by Kollen and Co. of Prague. The alternator was rated at 250kVa directly driven by a 375 horse-power impulse turbine whilst a second exciter was used to provide lighting and heating in the Kellow's house.

Transmission was at a nominal 3000 Volts, being transformed down to 220 Volts between phases for all purposes. Group driving for the quarry mills consisted of 10 horse-power squirrel cage motors. Each quarry chamber had two arc lamps, each of 2000 candle power, suspended overhead.

This scheme was an early example of the use of 3 phase AC power for quarrying purposes and all the credit must go to Moses Kellow's pioneering spirit.

At a later date, the Aber Artro Hydro-Electric Lighting and Power Works were proposed in an order cited as the Aber Artro Electricity Special Order 1923. Acting upon the instructions of Mrs MA Owen of Aberartro, Moses Kellow prepared the plans for an extensive hydro-electric scheme with transmission and distribution over an area extending from Harlech to Barmouth. The transmission lines were to operate at 10,000 Volts. Scheduled unit charges were to be as follows:

A) in respect of the quarters ending thirty-first March and December - for any amount up to 15 units, 15 shillings and for each unit over 15 units, one shilling.

B) in respect of the quarters ending thirtieth of June and September - for any amount up to 10 units, 10 shillings and for each unit over 10 units, one shilling.

Work on a dam was carried out and a pipeline laid. However, the scheme was opposed by the North Wales Power Company who had put forward a scheme for the whole of North Wales, Cheshire and Crewe. Although causing a financial loss to the promoters, the Aber Artro Special Order was not granted by the Government of the day.

Moses Kellow continued his involvement in the slate industry for many years and pioneered other innovations regarding slate working machinery including a drilling machine named appropriately as the "Kell-drill"[8].

In his later years Moses Kellow resided at the Park, Cheltenham and his house was named "Oakley" a somewhat curious choice perhaps, since it resembled closely the name of a well known Blaenau Ffestiniog slate mine and mining family.

Chapter 3

POWER STATIONS AND SCHEMES

Hydro-electric schemes in North West Wales were developed mainly for commercial purposes where developers invested money in the hope of making substantial profits. other schemes came to fruition solely to provide motive power for privately owned industrial concerns very often utilising existing sources of water power.

These schemes can be broadly categorised as:

- 3.1 Village and domestic supplies.
- 3.2 Individual industrial supplies.
- 3.3 Major developments.
- 3.4 Schemes where electricity was not the prime objective

3.1 Village and domestic supplies

These schemes provided electricity for domestic purposes in small communities although on occasion overlapping occurred when part of the power produced was used for example to drive a saw mill. The earliest scheme in Wales was probably that undertaken by Richard Edwards in Llanuwchllyn, which commenced operating in 1910. Other communities and especially individual farms did not receive the benefit of an electricity supply until the mid 1950's when the Merseyside and North Wales Electricity Board carried out its "rural electrification programme". This programme was not fully completed until 1968 and it is a curiosity that farms within eyesight distances of power stations such as Cwm Dyli which commenced generating electricity in 1906, were not connected to the distribution system until 50 or more years later.

As can be seen from the following table, the majority of consumers were household premises, farms being in the minority, one reason being the additional distribution costs involved in supplying these sometimes isolated premises.

The table gives examples of domestic supply schemes together with commencement dates:

Year Started	District	Distributor	Consumers	Water, Oil or Bulk
1910	Llanuwchllyn	A Edwards	100 houses 13 farms	W.O.
1913	Llwyngwril	Celynnin E.S. Company	195 houses 8 farms	W
1923	Dinas Mawddwy	Rowland Evans	120 houses 10 farms	W
1923	Trawsfynydd	Griffith Pugh	150 houses 2 farms	W
1924	Aberangell	J Norman Jones	160 houses 21 farms	W
1926	Penmachno	Mrs E Roberts	32 houses	-
?	Cerrigydrudion	E.S. Company	80 houses 1 farm	-
?	Aberllefenni	J R Jones	70 houses 2 farms	W
?	Arthog	H A Casson	46 houses 5 farms	W

Further details on some village schemes can now be noted.

Betws-y-Coed

Street lighting came to Betws-y-Coed via the local gas works. An Electricity Supply Order was granted to the Urban District Council in 1906 although the system was not converted to electricity until 1913 when the Urban Council combined a hydro-electric and domestic water supply scheme drawing water from Lake Elsi. The hydro-electric plant, located adjacent to the Hafod Las quarry was connected to an 8 inch supply pipeline from the lake and consisted of two 40kW turbine-alternator sets producing single phase AC at 2000 Volts, 50 cycles. Power supplies were transformed down to 500 Volts or 250 Volts whilst lighting supplies operated at 110 Volts. The local population at the time was 1070. Prices charged per unit were 6d (old pence) for lighting and 3d for power.

Estimated capital expenditure for the scheme was £3720 (equivalent to £15,000 in present day terms).

In April 1939, the North Wales Power Company took over the supply to Betws-y-Coed.

See following page for *Figure 6:* - Betws-y-Coed power station and water treatment works pipework arrangement.

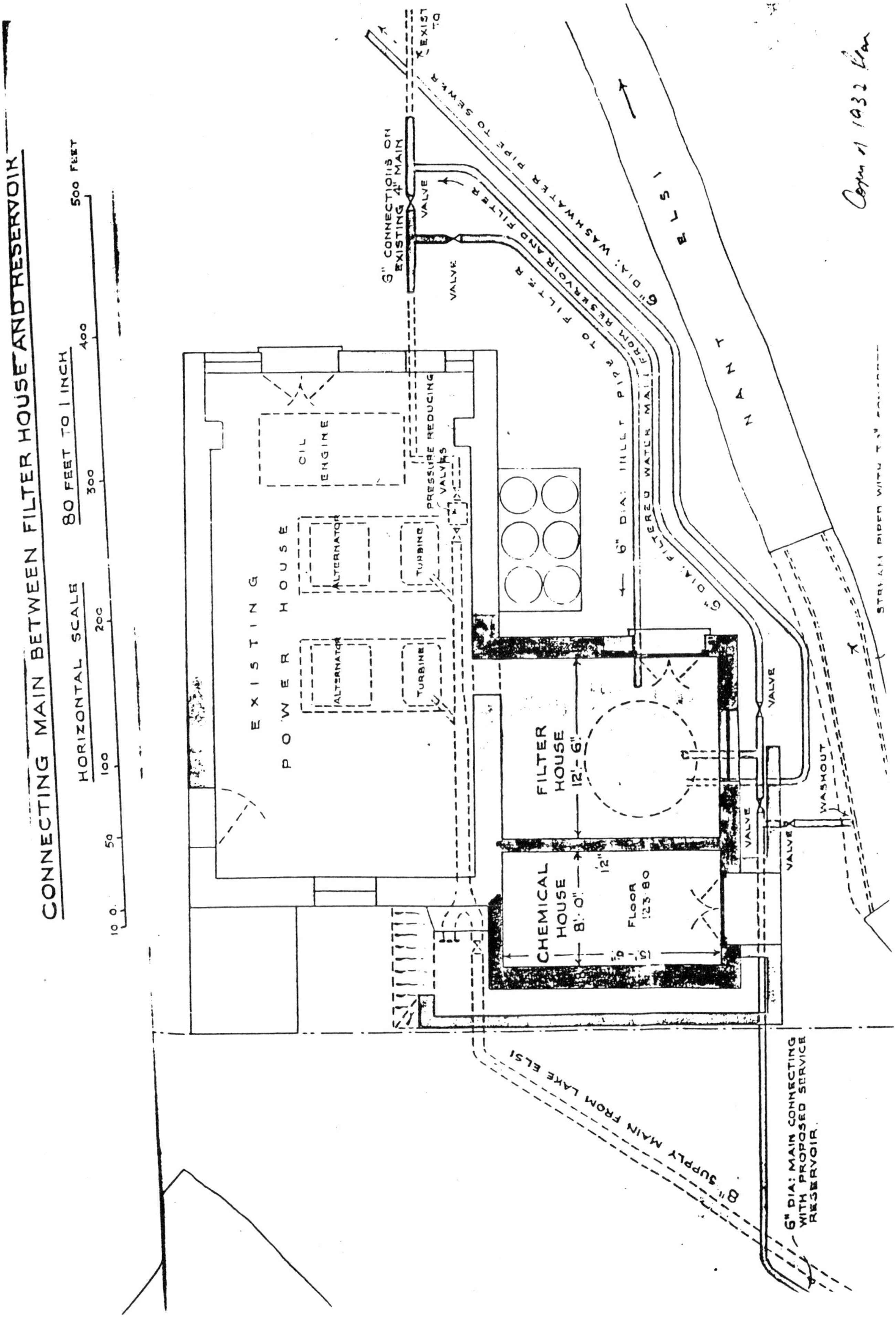
CONNECTING MAIN BETWEEN FILTER HOUSE AND RESERVOIR
HORIZONTAL SCALE
80 FEET TO 1 INCH
0 50 100 200 300 400 500 FEET
EXISTING POWER HOUSE
OIL ENGINE
ALTERNATOR
TURBINE
ALTERNATOR
TURBINE
PRESSURE REDUCING VALVES
FILTER HOUSE
12'-6"
CHEMICAL HOUSE
8'-0"
FLOOR 123·80
6" CONNECTIONS ON EXISTING 4" MAIN
VALVE
VALVE
6" DIA: WASHWATER PIPE TO SEWER
6" DIA: FILTERED WATER MAIN FROM RESERVOIR AND FILTER
6" DIA: INLET PIPE TO FILTER
NANT ELSI
WASHOUT
VALVE
VALVE
VALVE
8" SUPPLY MAIN FROM LAKE ELSI
6" DIA: MAIN CONNECTING WITH PROPOSED SERVICE RESERVOIR

Abergynolwyn

Abergynolwyn was part of the high quality slate producing area of the old Merionethshire, the Bryneglwys quarry product being comparable in quality with the Blaenau Ffestiniog slate. From 1866 until 1947, when the quarry closed, Bryneglwys slate was transported from Abergynolwyn via the narrow gauge railway to Tywyn. The Talyllyn railway was promoted by Lancashire cotton magnates being an investment opportunity at the time of the American Civil War.

In the 1860's the then quarry owners, the Aberdovey Slate Company, built 71 houses, mainly in the form of single fronted two-storey properties together with a general store, which formed the basis of the present day village[9].

By the time of the 1871 Census, 516 people were recorded as residing in the township of Maestrefnant between Rhiwenfa, Bryneglwys and the village of Abergynolwyn.

In 1901 the quarry employees numbered 174, which declined to 61 by 1931.

Following a period of closure, the quarry was re-opened under the auspices of the Abergynolwyn Slate and Slab Company Ltd, which was incorporated on 2nd November 1911. The sole director was Henry Haydn Jones, who also owned the railway. Neither the railway or the quarry were financially successful and were operated mainly to overcome high unemployment. Henry Haydn Jones later became the Member of Parliament for Merioneth and was also knighted.

At Pandy farm in Abergynolwyn, there was a building used as a saw mill with an overshot waterwheel driven by the waters of Nant Gwernol. In addition to powering the saw in the mill, the waterwheel also later drove a small dynamo. Haydn Jones installed a small hydro-electric plant in about 1923 to supply electricity to the village - to be used for lighting purposes only. He must have had great faith in Osram products because he stipulated that only Osram tested light bulbs were to be used. No individual meters were installed, the cost for electricity being included in the rental charges. There was to be not more than one 40Watt bulb in each living room and one 20Watt bulb in each bedroom. Ironing was permitted during specified 2 hour periods each week. The supply was interrupted if occupants used electrical heating. Low water flows during dry weather periods resulted in no supply being available at all. It has been recounted that an individual in charge of the switchboard would interrupt the supply at a specified time of an evening as a signal to his teenage daughter that it was time for her to return home.

Agergynolwyn was connected to the main distribution system in 1962.

Aberangell

Another instance of a combined operation facility was the installation at Aberangell where a non-statutory, privately owned undertaking supplied electricity for a saw mill and for private lighting and heating.

The supply at Aberangell in the upper Dyfi valley commenced on 1st October 1924 with plant comprising of one 20 horse-power turbine and one 30 horse-power turbine driving 14 kW EEC and 16 kW Crompton dynamos. Transmission was overhead at 200-240 Volts DC, the main system extending to 6 miles. There was also an auxiliary 20 horse-power crude oil engine installed.

The proprietor was J Norman Jones and the scale of charges were:- lighting, 8d per unit for the first 30 units: 5d per unit for the second 30 units; 3d for all units over 60. The number of consumers was 36. Maximum load was 60 amps. Public lighting consisted of six 60 Watt lamps.

Machynlleth

Machynlleth Electric Supply Company Limited was registered on 5th July 1932. A Special Order of 1932 granted to Arthur Lloyd Owen Owen and transferred to the company authorised supply within the urban district of Machynlleth and parts of the parishes of Isygarreg, Uwchygarreg and Penegoes, all in Montgomeryshire. The extent of the authorised area was 250 acres with a population approaching 2000 with 552 premises.

The Company negotiated for rights to extract and divert water on land occupied by the then owner of Plas Forge, Machynlleth and agreed as part of the compensation to supply Plas Forge with 100 units of electricity per annum for lighting purposes for the period of the lease. There were leases with a Mr Jarman and a Mrs Walker to construct dams across the river Dulas and a lease dated 13th February 1933 was made with Mr Edwin Evans allowing water to be transported over Mr Evans' land, the lease also allowing erection and maintenance of poles and wires for the transmission of electric current.

The power station was a combined water power and oil engine plant. Supply commenced in 20th February 1933.

The system was AC, 3 phase, 50 cycles, generated at 400 Volts with overhead transmission at 11,000 Volts and 3,300 Volts, distribution being at 400 Volts and 230 Volts. The hydro-electric side of the plant derived its water from a catchment area of 17½ square miles but only part of the available water was used. The river Dulas, flowing from the natural lake Glaslyn with a further tributary form lake Bugeilyn was the immediate source of supply and the station operated on the run of the river with a head of only 40 feet. The water was drawn from the river at a collecting weir and carried for about half a mile to the station in a metal box flume 4 feet wide by 2 feet high.

A serious fire destroyed the original station building in 1937 but a new brick built structure was constructed around the plant. This building contained two Francis water turbines supplied by Gilbert Gilkes and Gordon of Kendal, being of 110 horse-power and 35 horse-power respectively. The turbines drove Brush alternators with a terminal voltage of 400 Volts, one being of 66kW capacity running at 500 rpm, the other being of

23kW capacity running at 750 rpm. The switchgear consisted of an open back type panel operating at 400 Volts, 3 phase and neutral.
The station was connected to the local distribution system by two transformers of 300kVa capacity.

Photo 1: Machynlleth power station exterior view

The company's authorised capital amounted to £7,000 in £5 shares, however, by 1945 the capital expenditure stood at £15,927 whilst revenue from the sales of current, including meter rents was £5,291 (equivalent to £95,238 in today's terms).

Supply statistics for 1945 were as follows:

Units generated:	Oil 229,084;	Water 240,272
Total:		469,356
Units Sold:		404,097
Maximum load:		146kW
Station load factor:		36.6%
Number of consumers:		620

Number of public lamps: 8

The manager for many years was IW Williams of Plas Forge, Machynlleth who was to remain involved with hydro-electricity in North Wales well into the post nationalisation period.

The hydro sets at Machynlleth were taken out of commission in 1965 and all abstraction and diversion works were demolished except the river sluice gate works which were handed over to the Gwynedd River Authority for fish control purposes.

Photo 2: Machynlleth power station with the two hydro sets on the left . Open plan machinery!!

See following page for *Figure 7:* - Machynlleth power station location map.

Figure 7:

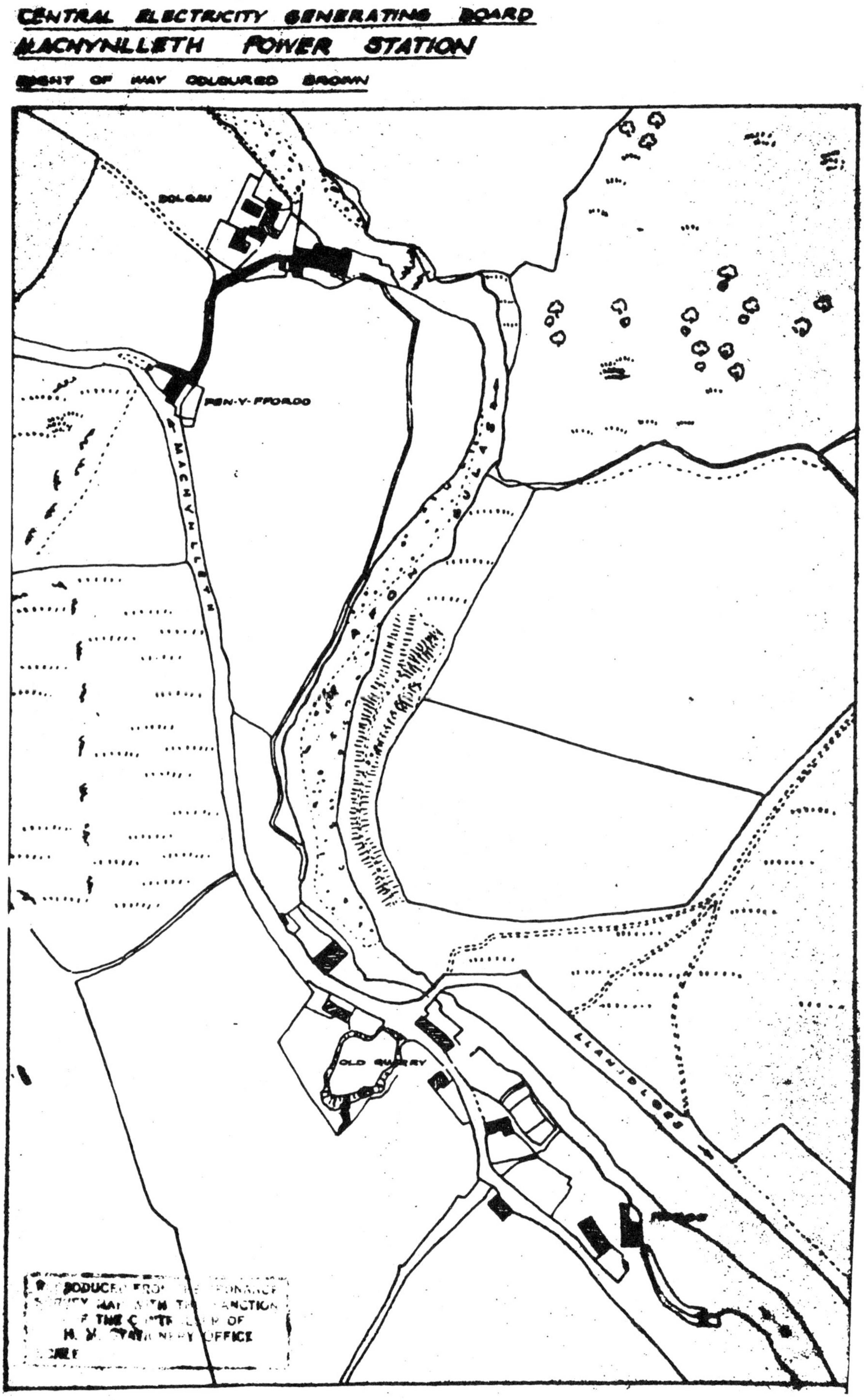
CENTRAL ELECTRICITY GENERATING BOARD
MACHYNLLETH POWER STATION
RIGHT OF WAY COLOURED BROWN
DOLGAU
PEN-Y-FFORDD
MACHYNLLETH
AFON DULAS
OLD QUARRY
LLANIDLOES

Towyn

Towyn and Aberdovey are small towns situated on the Cardigan Bay coast and adjacent to the estuary of the river Dovey in the former county of Merioneth.

The Towyn, Aberdovey and District Electricity Company Limited obtained a Special order under the provisions of the Electricity (Supply) Act 1882 to 1933 for the supply of electricity to and within the Urban District of Towyn and the neighbouring districts. The Company was formed and incorporated on 18th October 1934.

The power station comprised of two separate buildings set apart from one another on part of the defunct Felin-Llyn-Pair (Furnace lake mill) lead mines. The diesel engined station was situated on land purchased by the company on 7th October 1935 from RJ Corbett and others, the then owners of the adjoining Nant-y-Cynog farm. The hydraulic works were constructed and operated under the terms of a lease dated 12th August 1935, the parties being William Pugh and Annie Jones of Erwfaethlon farm near Towyn and John Alban Davies a surgeon of "Moranedd", Towyn, who was the "undertaker" for the Electricity Company. According to the terms of the lease, the Company were allowed to "take, appropriate, divert, lead, use and enjoy for all purposes in connection with their said Undertaking the water from Dyffryn Stream which passes over the lands of Erwfaethlon Farm aforesaid and from all and every the springs upon the said farm and to collect and convey the same waters into a dam and thence into and along the site of the old mill race there situate........ by means of pipes, troughings and other necessary apparatus....... and also full and free right and liberty to erect and place such pipes and fences on the land of the lessors as may be necessary from time to time".

The turbine house was erected downstream of the site of the diesel house and Messrs Gilkes of Kendal supplied a 50 horse-power set; governor and 110 feet of 18 inch diameter pipeline to the Company in 1935. As previously mentioned, the original head-race, part of the old mine workings was utilised, being extended by means of the pipeline to the turbine house.

The Company commenced the supply of electricity in June 1935, the plant installed being two 68 kW Brush diesel sets and one 34 kW Gilkes hydro set. Three further diesel sets were later installed but one was declared inoperable on 24th March 1961 because it was discovered that its foundation was directly over a suspect disused mine shaft.
The hydro set remained operational until the power station finally ceased to operate in 31st March 1965.

Before departing from Towyn and Aberdovey, it is worth noting that on 15th August 1921, a steam yacht entered the Dovey estuary and moored up at Aberdovey quay. The yacht was the Elettra, owned by no less a personage than Marconi, and that evening the local residents gathered on the quayside to hear music being broadcast from the Marconi wireless station at Waenfawr near Caernarfon, 40 miles away in a direct line. This wireless station at Waenfawr was supplied with electricity directly from the hydro-electric plant at Cwm Dyli power station details of which are given in a later section.

Figure 8:

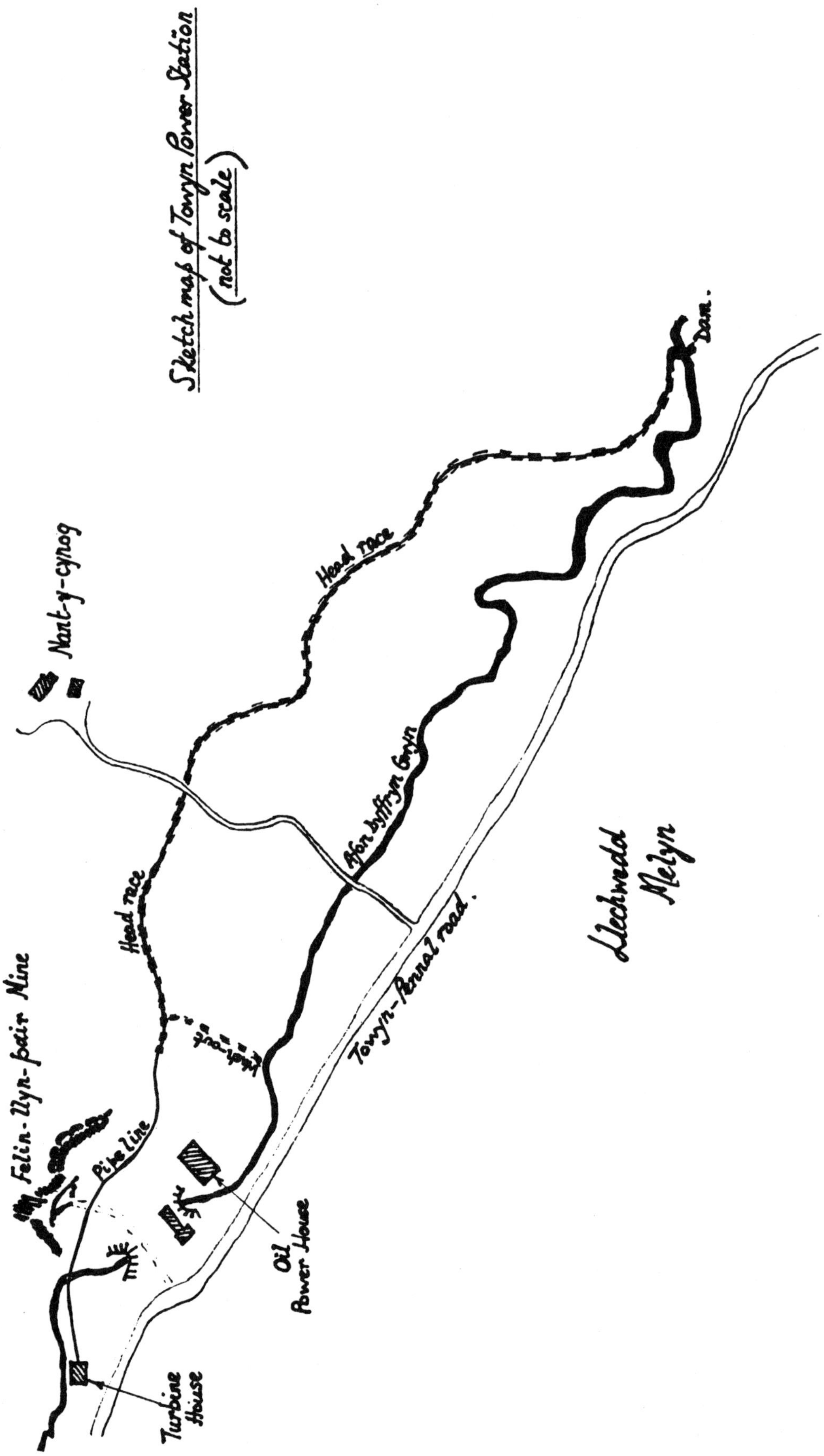
Sketch map of Towyn Power Station
(not to scale)
Dam.
Head race
Nant-y-cynog
Afon Dyffryn Gwyn
Head race
Felin-llyn-pair Mine
Pipe line
Oil Power House
Turbine House
Towyn-Pennal road.
Llechwedd Melyn

From the foregoing it is seen that hydro-electric schemes to provide supplies for villages and towns commenced with simple arrangements but very soon developed into relatively (for the area) sophisticated systems.

One factor which was common to all hydro systems was the longevity of the plant and this remains to be true up to the present day.

3.2 Individual Industrial schemes

These schemes, by definition, provided electricity solely for industrial purposes and were never envisaged as public supply facilities.

Llechwedd Quarry

The area around Blaenau Ffestiniog abounded with slate workings from very early times, some not developing any further than trial pits whilst others became large concerns and major employers. Between 1831 and 1881 the number of quarries increased from 7 to 20 and the population of the parish grew from 1,648 to 11,274. Blaenau Ffestiniog itself became the largest town in the old Merionethshire with over 4000 men employed in the slate quarrying industry at the end of the 19th Century.

The major quarries were the Oakeley, Votty and Bowydd and Llechwedd. The Llechwedd quarry was owned by the Greaves family having been purchased originally by John Whitehead Greaves (1807 - 1880) whose father was a banker in Leamington. The adjacent Maenofferen mine was also opened up by Greaves and eventually became another major site. At the present time both locations are worked jointly and an internal roadway links both sites, where high quality slate is still being produced.

Electricity first appeared at Llechwedd in 1891 when a dynamo, belt driven from a waterwheel was installed.

Photo 3: Llechwedd power station - Pant-yr-Afon power station, adjacent to the A470 road with the railway line from Llandudno Junction curving away to the right.

A hydro-electric power station was constructed at Pant-yr-Afon and commenced operation in October 1905, utilising water resources available in lakes benefiting from a high average annual rainfall. These lakes at Llyn Newydd; Bowydd; Barlwyd Bach and Barlwyd, via a system of leats, discharge water into Llyn Flags which is the commencement point of the pipeline feeding Pant-yr-Afon power house. Water from Llyn Newydd and Bowydd drives the plant at the Maenofferen power house.

Photo 4: Pant-yr-Afon - No 2 turbine generator set

Photo 5: Pant-yr-Afon - 28 November 1995 - a mere 90 years old!

Figure 9: Llechwedd Quarry - sketch of hydraulic system.

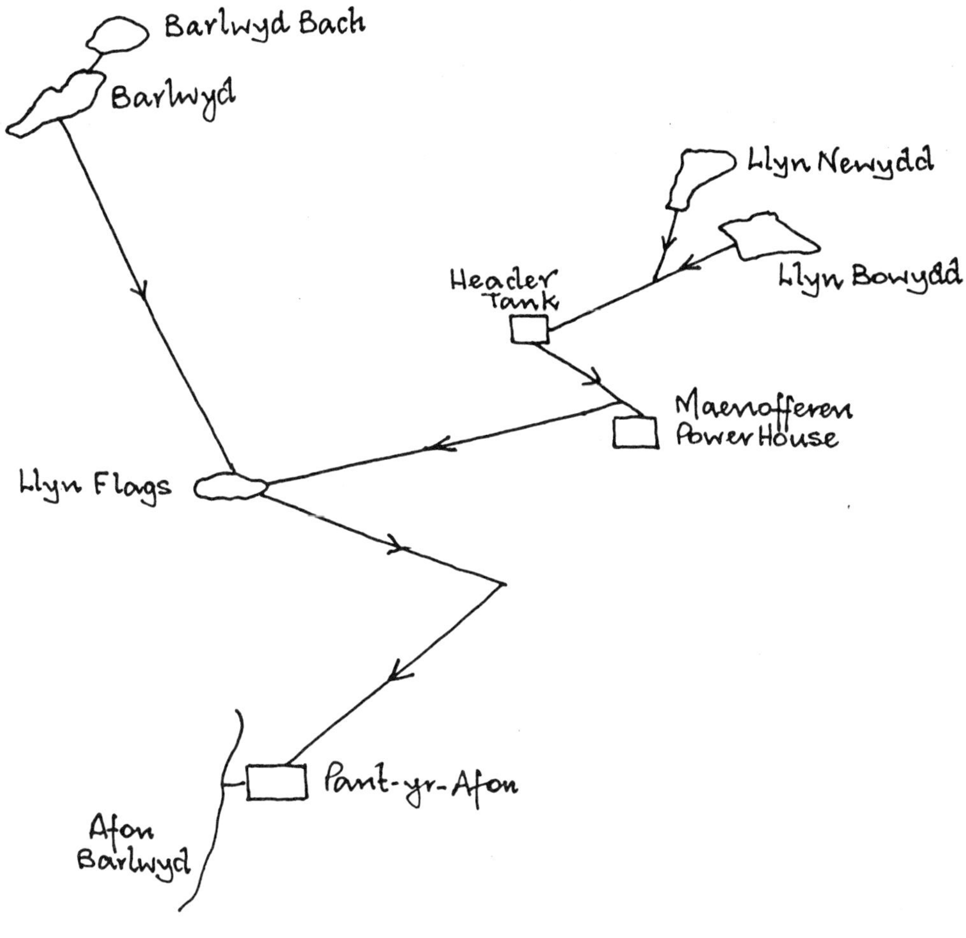

The pipeline to Pant-yr-Afon which is laid mainly over-ground is one mile long being of 18½ inch diameter as originally provided by Gilbert Gilkes and Gordon of Kendal in 1905. Repairs to the pipeline have ensured it has remained in good condition and a quotation from Horsely Bridge and Thomas Piggott Ltd of Tipton, Staffs. in 1954 (Z/DBE/350) for the supply of 18 lengths of lapwelded steel pipes of thickness varying from 1/4" to 3/8" amounted to £854. Presently as repairs become necessary, any new sections installed are of 20 inch diameter. The operating pressure of this system is 300 psi and there are five safety valves on the pipeline.

The power plant was installed to provide electricity for the quarry, ie lighting and power, a function that it still performs five days per week from 7.45am to 3.45pm each day Monday to Friday inclusive. Two single jet Pelton wheel turbines originally supplied by Gilbert Gilkes and Gordon each drive a Johnson and Philips DC generator rated at 250kW; 500 Volts, operating at a speed of 385 rpm. The turbine governors are belt driven from the main shaft regulating speed via the spear valves. An air pressure vessel connected to the pipeline within the station building is designed to absorb any shocks from pipeline surges. This vessel was originally pressurised by hand but now this function is achieved by a small engine driven compressor.

The plant is in excellent condition being well maintained. Maintenance over the years has included generator commutator skimming and turbine needle valve replacement. This proves yet again that properly maintained hydro plant has an exceptionally long life.

A report on the Llechwedd hydro plant (Z/DBE/3071)[10] dated 24th march 1921 states that the maximum load in 1906 was 300 Amperes whilst the average daily units taken were 700. By 1921 these amounts had increased to 700 Amperes and 2,400 units respectively.

The loading constituted the following parts:

Ffridd with 4 pumps working:	210 Amps
Floors 2 and 3:	160
Mills:	160
Main Winding:	130

(Short period incline loads could require 340 Amps)

In 1931, an agreement dated 4th September (Z/DBE/3076)[11] between the North Wales Power Co. Ltd., quoted for a supply of electricity in bulk from 1st October 1931 in the form of 3 phase alternating current at a nominal pressure of 400 Volts. The tariff was to be 1½d old pence (15p in present terms) per Board of Trade unit metered at low tension.

This external system supply provides power for pumping purposes and also acts as a back-up supply should the main generating plant not be available. If any surplus generation is produced, then energy is exported via the external system. A rotary converter is installed at Floor 5 which converts the DC supply into AC and also stabilises surges, especially when mill saws come on line. This unit, which is of English Electric manufacture, is rated at 420/460 Volts DC; 595/543 Amps and 311/341 Volts AC; 297 Amps; 6 phase, 50 cycles, 1500 rpm. It is at this point that the external supply enters into the quarry's system.

Photo 6: Pant-yr-Afon - makers plate affixed to a turbine casing and the air receivers prominent in the background.

Photo 7: Pant-yr-Afon - control panel and switchboard.

The Maenofferen power house is located at high level close to the mill complex and houses, a single turbine-generator and switchgear in a spacious building.

This turbine draws water only from Llyn Bowydd and Llyn Newydd via a header tank and operates at a pressure of 280 psi. the turbine, which is of the Turgo Impulse type was supplied by Gilkes of Kendal and has a speed of 550 rpm which directly drives a BTH DC generator rated at 257 kW; 460 Amps; 510 Volts no load and 570 Volts full load, and has 6 poles.

Photo 8: Llechwedd Quarry - Floor 5 rotary converter set and control gear. Incoming 415 Volt switchgear in the background.

Photo 9: Llechwedd Quarry - Booster House BTH rotary converter.

In the Booster House are two identical rotary converters supplied by BTH being of type HC and form CA having 6 phases, operating at 50 cycles, 1500 rpm and 1000 rpm respectively; 510Volts/392 Amps DC; 380 Volts AC; 200 kW.

The Maenofferen plant is also obviously well maintained and in good condition, and the author was privileged to witness its operation during a recent visit. This plant continues to fulfil its function and has been doing so for many years under arduous conditions.

Photo 10: Maenofferen turbine generator showing inlet pipe and valve associated with the Turgo impulse turbine.

As early as 1896, Llechwedd Quarry was described as being " in the way of machinery about the most up-to-date in the world" due mainly to the then manager Warren Roberts an engineer. Enhancements were made from 1919 when Captain Martyn Williams-Ellis AMIEE, AMIMechE, AMIME a member of the Greaves family, was appointed manager and engineer. A gas-oil engine generator was added at Pant-yr-Afon to cope with peak loads whilst two steam locomotives were converted to electrical drive with overhead pick-up.

Photo 11: Maenofferen power house - operational on 28th November 1995.

Photo 12: Maenofferen BTH DC generator.

Photo 13: Maenofferen - one of a pair of rotary converters.

Photo 14: Maenofferen converter house control panel and switchboard.

Trefriw Woollen Mill

The village of Trefriw, situated in the Conwy valley, once contained a flour mill, two breweries and two woollen mills, all situated to take advantage of the normally copious water flow in the River Crafnant. This river originated from Lake Crafnant and a tributary from Lake Geirionydd both lakes being situated in the parish of Llanrhychwyn.

The present Trefriw mill was purchased by Thomas R Williams in 1859. It had been functioning for at least 30 years prior to then and has been in the same family's ownership since 1859. TR Williams was a native of Rhydlydan in Merionethshire and the 1871 Census (RG10/5678.2)[12] gives the following information for the "factory":

Name	Relation to Head	Condition in Marriage	Age	Occupation	Where Born
Thomas Williams	Head	Married	30	Woollen Manufacturer	Rhydlydan, Merioneth
Ann Williams	Wife	Married	30	-	Trefriw
Thomas R Williams	Son		5	Scholar	Trefriw
Richard G Williams	Son		4	Scholar	Trefriw
Jane E Williams	Daughter		2	-	Trefriw
Ellen J Williams	Daughter		4mth	-	Trefriw
Mary Edwards	Servant	Single	15	Domestic Servant	Llanfairfechan
John Jones	Servant	Single	35	Weaver	
John Roberts	Servant	Single	15	Carder	

The mill was situated in the banks of the River Crafnant in order to use the water for washing the woollen cloth and for driving water wheels. These water wheels were dismantled in about 1900 when hydro-electric plant was first installed.

Photo 15: Trefriw Woolen Mill reservoir dam with water passing into the River Crafnant.

The River Crafnant is dammed above the village of Trefriw and a 20 inch diameter pipeline carries water to the two Boving pelton wheel turbines installed in the main mill building. The inlet pipes from the main pipeline to the turbine nozzles are of 12 inches diameter. The turbines operate under a net head of 60 feet being of the twin jet type running at a speed of 600 and 1000 revs per minute respectively. "V" belt driven pulleys drive the GEC alternators rated at 50 cycles, 0.8 power factor at 400 Volts. Total generating capadity is 60kW which is absorbed within the mill.

Photo 16: Trefriw Woolen Mill with the pipeline on the right. The main mill building is immediately behind the power line "H" pole.

Photo 17: Trefriw Woolen Mill - a portion of the power plant.

Of the present machines, one set was installed in 1933 and subsequently moved downstream to its present position in 1951. The second set was installed new in situ in 1942.

The Trefriw mills own the water rights relating to Crafnant and Geirionedd with water being stored overnight to provide sufficient quantities for daily operation. Regulating valves are operated to suit these requirements. Sufficient water was available during the drought of 1976 to enable half-laod generation all day every working day.

When the water industry was reformed nationally there came into being a body with the unwieldy title of Welsh National Water Development Authority (WNWDA) which was later separated into Welsh Water Authority and the National Rivers Authority (NRA). The NRA were given responsibility for water charging schemes relating to usage of water from varying sources, including privately owned sources. The charging schemes as originally envisaged would have meant that using water from Crafnant to generate electricity for the mill would have attracted exorbitant charges rendering the whole process uneconomic.
This applied to a slightly lesser degree to the major producers also, and caused great consternation. Some degree of common sense prevailed and the charging schemes were modified following consultations, allowing generation to continue.

The generating plant at the Trefriw mills can be seen in operation by visiting the mills during normal opening times.

Photo 18: Trefriw Woolen Mill - the water inlet pipes enter the buidling at a high level before bifurcating and curving down into the turbine

Photo 19: Trefriw Woolen Mill - the nearest belt drive is into the governor whilst the furthest is to the alternator.

Brynkir Woollen Mill

This mill is situated close to the popular and picturesque valleys of Cwm Pennant and Cwm Ystradllyn in the old Caernarfonshire. The mill was constructed for use as a corn mill but prior to 1850 was converted into a woollen mill. Originally motive power was provided by a water wheel, a feature found at countless other mills countrywide. Water was taken from the River Henwy which has its source in Lake Cwmystradllyn. The water wheel is still extant even though it is not used for its original purpose. The original hydro-electric plant which was installed to give a more efficient, modernised means of power was installed by none other than Richard Edwards of Llanuwchllyn, continuing to draw water from the river, the turbine being of Pelton wheel type. The present turbine was provided and installed by Gilkes of Kendal in 1946 and is rated at 21.5 horse-power operating under a head of 25 feet and revolving at 680 rpm. The system voltage is 415 Volts and the electricity provides lighting together with some machine driving within the mill.

Water requirements are 1.3 million gallons in 24 hours and since Lake Cwmystradllyn is also a public water supply reservoir with increasing demand to satisfy, especially to the large holiday complex near Pwllheli, the mill is also connected to the local electrical distribution system which provides power during low water flow periods.

3.3 Major Developments

Between 1899 and 1910, three major hydro-electric schemes were constructed in North West Wales which were followed by a fourth scheme which was completed in 1928.

These schemes were:

a) Dolwen (Yale Electric Power Company) at Blaenau Ffestiniog.
b) Cwm Dyli (North Wales Power & Traction Co. Ltd.) at Nant Gwynant near Beddgelert.
c) Dolgarrog (Aluminium Corporation Ltd) at Dolgarrog near Conwy.
d) Maentwrog (North Wales Power Company) at Maetwrog.

In later years, the combined generating capacity of these power stations was 58,789 kW or 58.789 MW and amounted to a major increase compared to the capacities of the schemes discussed earlier.

a) Dolwen

In a previous section it was noted that Thomas Parry Osborne Yale was instrumental in conceiving this scheme and forming the Yale Electric Power Company Limited.

The power station, known at different times as Dolwen or Ffestiniog power station, was to be situated on land which was leased to the Company by a Mr J L Jones. The lease dated February 17th, 1899 cites 'two pieces of land at Dolwen Farm, Festiniog with areas of one acre and two roods respectively' and gave the Power Company a number of rights. It had the right to divert and take all or any of the water from the River Goedol at the Dolwen falls and to convey such water by means of pipes to the power station site at which latter point all the water so diverted was to be restored and made to flow along the bed of the River Goedol. Secondly, it had the right to use water in any building erected on the piece of land two roods in area and it also had the right to lay pipes for the purpose of conveying water between the Dolwen Falls and the power station. Lastly it could erect, as required, poles or other appliances upon any part of Dolwen Farm. The lessor reserved several rights including the right to erect a bridge across the River Goedol at a point opposite the piece of land one acre in area; to cross the land (one acre in area) by means of a road made by the lessor and not less than 15 feet wide, to enable the lessor to obtain access to Dolwen Farm; to tap a water pipeline by means of a 2 inch pipe to convey water for the use of the lessor's sheep or cattle; and finally the right to tap a main water pipeline by means of a 1 inch pipe, for the water to be used for any purpose.

A further lease existed for this undertaking with the Canon Haygarth Estate and related to a wayleave for diminution of water flow on about 380 lineal yards of land along the left bank of the Afon Goedol from the vicinity of the power station and upstream.

Water for the scheme was to be drawn from four lakes, namely Conglog, Cwm Corsiog, Cwmorthin and Stwlan, the first named being at an altitude of 2,002 feet OD, the highest in the scheme. The catchment area was 3 square miles in extent with an annual rainfall in the order of 90 inches.

Llyn Conglog, the most northerly of the four lakes, had a short, low dam constructed across the outlet stream on the southern side in 1899. The dam was twenty yards in length consisting in section of an upstream dry stone pitched wall 6 feet thick by some 8 feet in height, behind which was a peat fill about 6 feet broad with a further 11 feet thickness of stone pitched walling forming the down stream side of the dam. At the eastern end of the dam a rough spillway of about 6 feet in width was provided. A culvert 2 feet by 1½ feet through the walls and peat led to an 18 inch outlet pipe discharging into the river. The reservoir area at top water level was 19 acres with a storage value of approximately 13,500 kilowatt-hours through the power station.

Llyn Corsiog, a smaller reservoir than Conglog, was further to the west with a surface area of about 8 acres. In this case there were two dams at the south end of the lake constructed in 1899, the larger being 170 feet in length and about 15 feet maximum height with a narrow spillway at one end. An 8 inch diameter pipe through the dam provided a supply of water to the Rhosydd slate quarry about a mile distant. The spillway was furnished with a gate with two openings of 3 inches each as the entrance to a leat to the slate quarry, the water being utilised for power run onto an overshot water wheel. The second dam was 70 feet in length and 8 feet maximum depth of water furnished with a 12 inch diameter pipe through the wall for power water draw-off purposes. Both dams were solid dry stone pitched, the larger being 12 feet thick and the smaller 9 feet thick and both with a timber facing on the upstream side to make them watertight.

Conglog and Corsiog discharged via the rivers into Llyn Cwmorthin, a natural lake of approximately 24 acres from which storage was obtained by constructing an outlet below the natural ground and without the construction of any artificial barrier to raise the top water level thus giving an actual draw-off of 4 feet through a covered channel 3 feet square. Cwmorthin was owned by the Oakeley Quarries Ltd over two thirds of its area and the remaining one third was owned by a Captain Matthews who also owned the ground on which Llyn Conglog and Llyn Corsiog were situated.

Llyn Stwlan, a natural lake, was formed into a reservoir of 10 acres in area and had a composite wall of dry pitched stone and peat as described for Llyn Conglog. The original spillway was at one end of the dam at a level of 1,582 feet O.D. Stwlan was leased from three owners, The Crown, Lord Harlech and OL Owen.

Whilst Llyn Conglog and Llyn Corsiog both discharged into Llyn Cwmorthin to the south-west as already stated, Llyn Stwlan was south of the main gathering ground and discharged into Afon Stwlan and Afon Cwmorthin, tributaries of Afon Goedol on which the power station was situated. Discharges from all the reservoirs were manually controlled. The total storage capacity of the reservoirs amounted to 14 million cubic feet.

A further dam was situated on the Afon Goedol about 700 yards upstream of the power station holding back water in the river and forming a forebay to the pressure pipes leading to the power station, the head of water available being 200 feet. The dam was constructed across a deep and narrow gully and was 30 feet high and some 20 feet maximum bottom width of solid masonry in a natural hole formed by the action of the water in the rock of the stream bed. On several occasions it was known to have 5 feet of water on the crest of the dam. The capacity of the forebay was 200,000 cubic feet.

The pipeline from the forebay to the power station was of steel and 2 feet in diameter except near the head of the line, where, owing to difficulties of carriage at the time of construction, a double line of 18 inch pipes was used.

The plant consisted originally of two 9kW generators manufactured by the Sandycroft Foundry Company of Chester operating at 560 volts and each directly coupled to a water turbine.

Photo 20: Dolwen power station exterior with water discharging into the river from the tailrace.

The Company gave a 24 hour supply. providing power to the slate mines and quarries for hauling, pumping and mill driving and also electric lighting for the town streets and private consumers.

Before the introduction of electricity into the mines steam was used for the same purpose and one of the conditions imposed on the contractors was that the conversion from steam to electrical driving should be carried out without stoppage of work, and that the existing starting handles of the winding engines should be retained. The old gearing was consequently used in most cases and the steam plant remained in position. It was possible, therefore, by simply shifting the driving pinions, to run by steam power in cases of emergency thus saving the cost of spare armatures and other vital parts of the electrical portion of the machinery.

Power was supplied to the large consumers at one penny per unit and the first mines to benefit by this low charge were Votty and Bowydd and Messrs Greaves and Sons. The company also entered into an agreement with the Urban District Council to supply electricity for public and private lighting at a maximum rate of 4 pence per unit for a period of 15 years. This is believed to be the first time that a public electricity supply had been produced by water power in Great Britain, and on 22 May 1902, Lord Newborough performed the ceremony of inaugurating the public supply.

Energy was supplied at 500 volts for power purposes and at 230 volts for lighting, heating and small motors. The company undertook the mines pumping by contract, enabling it to supply power for this purpose at the most convenient times to itself for equalising the load on the generators.

By 1902, motors to the extent of 400 horsepower were actually connected to the mains together with 3,000 lamps or their equivalent besides about a dozen arc lamps for lighting the streets and the goods yard of the Great Western Railway which was the only station on their Chester division to be lighted electrically.

Photo 21: Dolwen power station plant and main swithchboard.

The generating plant in 1902 consisted of two 'Sandycroft' 6 pole, continuous current generators each capable of an output of 90KW at 560 volts direct coupled one on each side by means of 'Sandycroft' flexible couplings to a double Pelton wheel turbine with 4 nozzles. A battery of the 'Tudor' type was installed of 140 ampere-hours capacity at the one-hour discharge rate. The battery was worked in conjunction with the generators, the load on the latter being kept practically constant by means of a differentially wound motor booster. The arrangement was automatic; the generators charged the battery on light load and on heavy loads the generators and battery supplied current in parallel to the line.

The generators were separately excited by a dynamo, direct driven by a small Pelton wheel turbine, but by means of suitable arrangements on the switchboard they could be made self-exciting if desired. The motor driving the booster could also be driven by a turbine as a generator and was intended for use as an auxiliary machine for light loads or for charging up the battery if necessary when the main generators were shut down. The main switchboard consisted of two generator panels and battery, exciter and distribution panels.

The transmission line consisted of three overhead circuits of bare hard-drawn copper cable carried on insulators of the double-petticoat type. The circuits could be worked independently or in parallel and from the power station the overhead line conveyed current to the slate mines, the distance being 3,500 yards. Double pole construction was principally employed for the main line thus ensuring a wide margin of safety even under the very trying conditions to be met with in this part of the country. A telephone line was also provided.

At the Votty and Bowydd mine, a 150 b.h.p., Robey winding engine was driven by a 6 pole 'Sandycroft' motor, driving a drum shaft through gearing. The shaft carried three drums used for winding up an incline 200 yards in length. There was also installed an 80 b.h.p., 4 pole 'Sandycroft' motor driving two drums by means of belting and gearing winding up an incline also of 200 yards in length. At the same mine was another 80 b.h.p., 4 pole motor driving two drums through gearing for a 400 yard incline. These motors were all provided with the 'Sandycroft' special type of magnetic brake. For pumping there was a set of three-throw- horizontal pumps capable of lifting 160 gallons of water per minute to a height of 350 feet and a second set of pumps of the same type capable of lifting 50 gallons under a head of 400 feet.

From the Votty and Bowydd mine, a line branched off for a distance of 900 yards to Messrs. Greaves and Sons mine where a 10 b.h.p. semi-enclosed motor drove a mill etc, and for sinking operations at these mines a 'Sandycroft' semi-portable electric winch was used, driven by a totally enclosed motor.

In the town of Blaenau Ffestiniog, lying between the power station and the mines, through which the high pressure mains passed, a sub-station was erected, where a motor-generator of 40KW capacity was installed and this reduced the voltage, which for public and private lighting was 230 volts at the consumer's terminals. This sub-station also contained the local offices of the company and occupied a central position. The day lighting load was taken by a Tudor battery of 90 ampere-hours capacity at the 3 hour discharge rate and the motor-generator was controlled and distribution affected by a switchboard, consisting of a high pressure panel and motor-generator, battery and feeder panels. An extensive system of telephones was employed, the central point being the town sub-station.

In 1937, a major change took place, whereby the 500 volts D.C. system was dispensed with to be replaced by A.C. generation at 400 volts, including the installation of two alternators of English Electric Company's manufacture in the power station, together with switchgear rated at 11,000 volts.

The average annual units generated 1938-1948 were 2,045,000 KWH. In 1948 over 2,700,000 KWH were generated. Cwmorthin was open a total of 407 hours and Conglog was emptied on two occasions to replenish Cwmorthin. 1948 could be termed a wet year. During a normal year Conglog was emptied 5 or 6 times.

Plant installed in the power station in 1949 was as follows:-

Plant Item	*Particulars*
Gilkes & Gordon, Turgo turbine	200ft head: 20hp date unknown: out of service
Boving, Pelton wheel turbine	200ft head: 300hp: 1928
Escher Wyss, Francis horizontal turbine	200ft head: 600hp: 1899
Sandycroft D.C. dynamo	750 rpm 230-265 Volts: 130 Amps: 1902
English Electric Alternator	437KVA: 600 rpm: 400 Volts 368 Amps: 1937
English Electric Alternator	255KVA: 300 rpm: 400 Volts 368 Amps: 1937
English Electric cubicle switchgear	O.C.B.: 11KVA: 25 Amps: 1937 O.C.B.: 11KV: 15 Amps: 1937 O.C.B.: 11KV: 30 Amps: 1937
English Electric Tansformers	500KVA: 33KV/11KV 440KVA: 11,000/400 Volts 250KVA: 11,000/400 Volts
D.C. circuit breakers	2 x 200 Amps
D.C. exciters	43 Volts: 135 Amps 28 Volts: 196 Amps

Costs for 1953/54 for Dolwen power station were:-

Total works costs	4002
Rental payable on Lloyd Jones lease	250
Rental payable on Haygarth lease	35
	£4287

Cost per unit generated = 0.358 pence

The original company had handed over its undertaking to a Birmingham based concern in 1936 and they later handed over to the Ridgeway Trust Ltd, of 9 Clarges Street, London who owned the scheme at vesting date in 1948. When the Ffestiniog pumped storage scheme was constructed by the C.E.G.B. at Tanygrisiau in 1957-8 the lower reservoir for the new scheme was created by constructing a dam across the natural outlet of the basin of Afon Ystradau which cut off the natural flow into Afon Goedol and the forebay of Dolwen power station. Thereafter the smaller station only produced power when excess water was released through the discharge regulators on the lower dam of the pumped storage scheme.

When the leases became due for renewal, the C.E.G.B. did not take up the options and Dolwen power station finally ceased operating on 31st March 1964.

b) Cwm Dyli Power Station

The next major development in North Wales was Cwm Dyli power station, situated 1½ miles east of Snowdon summit (3,560 feet). Attention had been focused on the possibilities of developing the natural water resources in this area some years before the turn of the century when far-seeing pioneers formed a company named Gwalia Limited and acquired all the important water rights of Snowdonia, their freehold land extending from the Conwy valley to the western slopes of Snowdon. Unfortunately support was lacking and the company was unable to carry out its development. Part of the water rights were sold to a company called the North Wales Power and Traction Company Limited, of which Sir Thomas Beecham was chairman. The Cowlyd lake above the Conwy valley was sold to the Conway and Colwyn Bay Joint Water Supply Board and the remainder of the lands and water rights by auction to various buyers.

The North Wales Power and Traction Company Ltd., with full co-operation of the landowners, Baron Hill Estate, developed the water power on a portion of Snowdon by constructing the works at Cwm Dyli; the Portmadoc, Beddgelert and South Snowdon Railway Company was formed and partly constructed a railway from South Snowdon towards Portmadoc designed to use electrical power but failed to complete; the Snowdon Mountain Tramroad and Hotels Company was formed and built a rack railway to the summit of Snowdon but failed to use the hydraulic power opting instead for steam locomotives constructed in Switzerland.

In the North Wales Electric Power act of 1904 the North Wales Power and Traction Company was authorised to supply electric power in bulk and for power purposes within an area comprising the then four North Wales counties of Caernarfon, Merioneth, Anglesey and part of Denbigh.

The construction work of the scheme at Cwm Dyli for generating power from Llyn Llydaw and the watersheds of the Snowdon range began in 1905, the main contractor for the whole scheme being Messrs Bruce Peebles and Co Ltd of Edinburgh whilst the consulting engineers were Sir Douglas Fox and Partners and Messrs Harper Brothers. Great difficulties were experienced during the construction especially of the pipeline, due to the location, terrain and climate conditions and it was necessary to construct several incline haulage's to haul pipes, ballast, concrete etc into position. Three traction engines and numerous horse haulages were employed to bring heavy loads over the Llanberis pass from Llanberis railway station some eight miles distant and mule teams also played their part in transporting machinery, pipes and poles. Over 800 men were employed on the construction of the pipelines and power station whilst hundreds of others were engaged on the transmission lines and sub-stations.

Photo 22: Cwm Dyli power station - transmission lines construction material in the railway yard at Llanberis, a traction engine, a car and a locomotive are visible.

Photo 23: Cwm Dyli power station - horse haulage on purpose laid tramway during construction in 1905.

Commercial supply of electricity commenced on 13 August 1906 and the power station has been in continuous operation since that date.

The Cwm Dyli hydro-electric scheme was an outstanding achievement at the time as it had one of the highest operating heads at 1,124 feet and as originally planned a generating pressure of 10,000 volts with power transmission by overhead lines.

The catchment area is remarkably small at 1,000 acres but has a high annual rainfall, the average for 1963-1983 being 162 inches whilst the highest recorded annual rainfall was 212 inches in 1954. The lowest recorded annual rainfall at the Copper Mine was in 1941 and amounted to a paltry 105 inches! Storage was provided in Llyn Llydaw, a natural lake, and a stone and cement dam was constructed with wooden stop-logs to increase the spillway height and created a reservoir with a storage capacity of 145 million cubic feet. The development by the Power Company was not the first industrial activity in this remote location as the Britannia* Copper Mine had their works on the northern side of Llyn Lydaw. The intake works in Llyn Llydaw for the scheme were constructed with the assistance of the Tilbury Contracting and Dredging Co Ltd and consists of a 4 feet diameter cast iron pipe laid in a 5'6" channel with sloping sides running out to a distance of 180 feet from the shoreline into the lake. The intake pipe led into a wet chamber in the intake tower, a concrete structure, where there was also an upper inlet, 3 feet square at 5 feet below OHWM. The dry chamber in the intake tower housed an isolating valve that controlled the flow of water into a 3'6" diameter concrete lined tunnel which after 500 feet bifurcated into two tunnels, each 2'6" in diameter which connected with two 30" diameter steel pipelines. An isolating, manually operated valve was provided on each pipeline 120 feet downstream of the tunnel exit and an isolating valve on each pipeline adjacent to the power station building, together with a valve situated in the pipe race at the side of the building to give an interconnecting facility between the two pipelines.

Photo 24: Cwm Dyli power station - steam powered winch for pipeline construction located close to the miners track and to the point where the pipeline low to high pressure transition occurs.

Pipeline dimensions were as follows:-

Low pressure section : 30 inch diameter:

1000 feet, single riveted 9/32" thick.
500 feet, double riveted 9/32" thick.
1500 feet, double riveted 5/16" thick.
1320 feet, double riveted 11/32" thick.

High pressure section: 27 inch diameter forge lap welded:

486 feet, 3/8" thick.
486 feet, 7/16" thick.
486 feet, 1/2" thick.
486 feet, 9/16" thick.
252 feet, 5/8" thick.

* 1907 - Electricity generated by a waterwheel is said to have powered the dressing floors and the crushing plant was powered by a Pelton wheel under a 550 feet head of water conveyed by pipeline from Glaslyn[13].

Photo 25: Cwm Dyli power station - as constructed

The original plant installed in the power station comprised of four generating sets numbered 1, 2, 3 and 4 and consisted of identical 1500kVa, 3 phase alternators by Bruce Peebles generating 3 phase current, 50 cycles at 10,000 Volts with direct coupled exciters, driven by 1,600 horse-power Pelton wheel turbines by Ganz. Each turbine was provided with a governor control which actuated a small auxiliary valve for controlling the movement of a piston in a hydraulic cylinder, the piston movement being communicated to the nozzles by means of a simple lever system. When the governor deflected the jets away from the turbine runner buckets they impinged on a baffle plate supported by angle irons and backed by timbers before falling into a pool of water in the tailrace. This baffle was sometimes subjected to the force of fully deflected jets at 500lb/in^2 and on one occasion prior to the installation of this feature, the jet of water bored its way through 4 feet of concrete in a short space of time.

The plant was first run on test in July 1906 and the power station commenced supplying electricity on 13 August, 1906. Supply feeders in 1906 were Nantlle, Llanberis, Ffestiniog and Dolgarrog and large consumers included The Oakeley Slate Quarry co. Ltd., Blaenau Ffestiniog; The Pen-yr-Orsedd Slate Quarry Co. Ltd., Nantlle; The Dinorwic Quarries, Llanberis and The Penrhyn Quarries, Bethesda. In 1910 a further supply feeder was commissioned, namely Marconi, to provide power to the Marconi Wireless Telegraph Co. Ltd., station at Waenfawr. Plant changes occurred over the years, a fifth generating set, numbered 5, was installed in 1920, having a single Pelton wheel turbine running at 500rpm and a Peebles alternator of 2,000kVa which commenced operation in June 1921. No 4 set ceased operation in 1928, the last recorded running being on 15 November that year and the set was dismantled in June 1934. Also in 1934, on 26 November, a new No 3 set was put in commission replacing the original machine of the same number. This new set No3 had a Boving single Pelton wheel turbine running at 600 rpm and a 3,5000kVa Peebles alternator. The plant capacity at this time was two sets of 1,000kW each (No 1 & 2), one set of 3,000kW (No 3) and one set of 1,5000kW (No 5).

The switchgear was located in a room adjoining the main machine hall and opening onto it, consisting of a rectangular steel bar cage with switch panels on two opposite sides and protective wire grilles on the other two. The panels were of white marble; six machine panels, four of which were equipped, faced on to the generators; the remaining panels - facing the outer wall of the switch room - six feeders, two spares and two summation panels. The switch equipment was sub-contracted to Messrs Ferranti, the generator panels contained the operating handle of the main oil switch with overload trip coils mounted below; there were five instruments on the upper part i.e. ammeter, voltmeter, watt meter, exciter and synchronising voltmeters and field switches on the lower part.

The feeder board consisted of ten panels, six being for feeders, two spares and two summation panels. The panels contained the handle of the feeder oil switch with the overload trip coils below, and two ammeters and an indicating lamp above. Bare copper leads carried on porcelain insulators ran through the basement from the generators to the oil circuit breakers and from there led up through isolating links to 'ring' bus-bars of 1 inch by ¼ inch copper supported by porcelain insulators on the bar-frame above. The feeder connections were taken from the opposite half of the 'ring'. Isolating links were provided in the bus-bars between all feeder and generator connections. From the bus-bars, the feeder connections passed down to the feeder oil switches which were provided with an alarm bell in connection with the tripping coils giving a warning if a feeder tripped out. From the oil switches, the outgoing feeders rose out above the board and passed through choking coils - in connection with horn lightning arrestors just above - and down through a series of rectangular openings in the wall of the building to a straining frame outside which formed the starting point of the overhead transmission.

Telephonic communication was provided along all the transmission lines and up to the intake structure at the reservoir, the instruments being of a special pattern by Deckert and Homolka of Prague and were designed to prevent the possibility of shock to the user.

Altogether 26 miles of transmission lines operating at 10,000 Volts were erected. One three-phase line, consisting of three 8mm wires, ran as straight as an arrow in an easterly direction from the station, up over 'Y Cribau' to a point near Roman Bridge where it turned south and terminated at the Oakley Quarries in Blaenau Ffestiniog, a distance of 7 miles. This transmission line was identified as 'Line 1' and the employee responsible for patrolling and maintaining this line for many years was known as 'Bob No 1' or 'Bob Polion' (Bob the poles) whose sideline was making coffins. This line was dismantled a few years ago but its route up the mountainside is still discernible. The principle transmission consisted of 3 three-phase lines, each consisting of 9mm wires, turned north from the power station subsequently passing in a westerly direction over the Llanberis pass, where a 6mm line branched off to the right to Messrs Asheton Smith's Dinorwic Quarries. The main transmission here turned south, climbing over the shoulder of Snowdon, some 2300 feet above sea level and dropped on the other side to Cwellyn lake where it crossed the North Wales Narrow Gauge Railway. From this point the transmission line turned westward, terminating at the Pen-y-Orsedd Quarries at Nantlle. As in the construction of the power station, many difficulties were encountered in the pole line work, the latter indeed, necessitating the laying down of temporary tram roads of which some 10 miles were used, for hauling the materials over boggy ground.

The high voltage transmission lines were numbered sequentially starting with Line 1 to the Substation at Oakeley Quarries. Line 2 took a route over Pen-y-Pass and down to the Dinorwic Quarries and was double circuit. If one travels along the present day road, soon after leaving Pen-y-Pass, travelling towards Nant Peris, there is still remaining a concrete block with a portion of steel transmission line tower.

Line 3 went on from Llanberis to the Nantlle quarries, whilst Line 4 took a route from Cwm Dyli along Dyffryn Mynibyr to Llyn Cowlyd originally to provide power during the construction of the dam at that location. This line later continued as a direct connection to Dolgarrog power station.

Line 5 ran through the Gwynant valley to a substation close to Llanfrothen, from where links were later made with Maentwrog power station and the town of Portmadoc.

Line 6 was an extension to Line 3 at Drws-y-Coed and Line 7 carried on from Lower Dinorwic over the mountains to Penrhyn Quarry at Bethesda.

Line 8 proceeded from Llanberis to the Waenfawr area, specifically for the Marconi Radio Station.

As previously stated, the main transmission voltage was originally 10,000 volts, however, subsequently a 3,000kVa: 10/20kV transformer was installed for transmission to the general system and on the 20kV switchboard served by the transformer were units controlling outgoing supplies to Dolgarrog, Llanfrothen and Caernarfon. A seven-panel, Reyrolle iron-clad type switchboard controlled the individual generator outputs and the outgoing 10kV circuits.

From 1906 to 1918, the North Wales Power Company's system was supplied entirely from Cwm Dyli power station.

Photo 26: Cwm Dyli power station - interior 1906

Cwm Dyli Power station - Costs for October 1906

Generation	
Oil, waste etc.	16-11
Tools, brushes etc.	£1-13- 8
Wages	£29-12- 6
Structural Repairs	
Materials	8- 9½
Tools	1- 9½
Wages	£3- 8- 1
Turbine Repairs	
Materials	11- 6
Wages	14-10
Transmission Line Inspection	
Wages	£13-15- 8
Transmission Line Repairs	
Wages	7- 8½
Pipeline Inspection	
Wages	£4- 5- 1
Intake Repairs	
Materials	10½
Wages	3- 6

Figure 10: - Cwm Dyli trading account for June 1910. The amount shown against S.S. is the Superintendent's monthly salary:

Backwood Power House

The North Wales Power and Traction Co., Ltd.

Works Cost for Month ending June 30th 1910

EXPENDITURE.	£	s.	d.	£	s.	d.	£	s.	d.
GENERATION. S. S.				12	10	-			
Wages and Gratuities (Power House				45	0	3			
Wages and Gratuities (~~Pipe Line~~ Ac. Road				6	3	6			
Oil, Waste and Engine-room Stores				-	19	5			
Repairs and Maintenance:—									
(1)—Buildings	-	4	2	1	8	10			
(2)—Turbines and Governors	1	11	11						
(3)—Generators and Exciters	-	-	5				69	8	10
(4)—Switchboard and Instruments	-	3	-						
(5)—Other Machinery, Instruments & Tools	-	10	7						
(6)—Pipe Line and Intake	-	16	9						
	3	6	10	3	6	10			
DISTRIBUTION.									
Wages and Gratuities				14	19	0			
" " T. & T.L. Extension a/c Pen-y-Pass				-	6	8			
" Linemen's Expenses				-	5	4			
Repairs and Maintenance									
Transmission and Telephone Line Materials				1	1	7	21	10	1
Transformers, Meters, Switches, Fuses and other Apparatus on Consumers' Premises				4	17	6			
Cartage and Haulage							-	16	3
							91	15	2
Surplus over Works Cost							217	0	8
							£308	15	10

NOTE.—Management Expenses are not included in Statement above.

REVENUE.	UNITS.	Rate	£	s.	d.
Oakeley	47800	7/8.	174	5	5
Pen-yr-Orsedd	16960	1d.	70	13	4
Dinorwic	8417	1½.	52	12	1
Pen-y-Gwryd.	665	} 3	7	10	-
Pen-y-Pass	160		3	15	-
TOTALS	74002	£	308	15	10

Total Units Generated ... 84170

" " Sold ... 74002

Average Price obtained per Unit Sold ... 1·00143.

Cost per Unit sold in pence	
Wages	0·26165
Oil, Waste and Engine Room Stores	0·00314
Repairs and Maintenance	0·03014
Cartage	0·00263
TOTAL	0·29756.

COMPARISON.

	THIS YEAR. Month.	THIS YEAR. 6 Months.	LAST YEAR. Month.	LAST YEAR. 6 Months.
	June	to June 1910	June	to June 1909
Units Sold	74 002	389 588	73 065	441 550
Average Price				
Revenue	£308 : 15 : 10	£1591 : 3 : 3	£302 : 5 : 5	£1833 : 12 : 10
Surplus over Works Cost	£217 : 0 : 8	£1067 : 15 : 6	£175 : 14 : 5	£1279 : 9 : 7

per GKP

The station superintendents of Cwm Dyli are given below, together with approximate dates in office:

1906-1909	Mr Harold Hinks
1909-1919	Mr Arthur Lockwood
1919-1921	Mr D Williams
1921-1930	Mr Richard K Hartley
1930-1944	Mr William Hwfa Williams
1944-1952	Mr E Salisbury Williams
1953-1963	Mr Charles H Williams

In 1961, Cwm Dyli power station together with Maentwrog and Dolgarrog power stations became part of the Ffestiniog Hydro Group.

Later changes saw transmission line voltages rated at 11kV and 33kV and at the intake works in Llyn Llydaw, the manually operated isolating valve situated in the dry chamber was replaced by an automatic self closing valve which was initiated to close at greater than normal full load water flow to afford protection in the event of a downstream pipeline failure.

All the turbines were provided with replacement Boving governors for speed control purposes and after many years service the generator switchgear was replaced with units rated at 11kV directly linked to the 11kV transmission switchgear via a bus-coupler circuit breaker. This arrangement proved troublesome on many occasions when electrical storms were active in the area.

There were no interposing transformers between the generators and the transmission system, and lightning strikes frequently came to earth in the alternator causing damage to the stator windings. The majority of the repair work was carried out by the station's staff and it was only damage of a more major nature that necessitated the presence of specialist repairers.

The plant at Cwm Dyli gave relatively trouble free service for many years, but by the early 1960's it was found that the pipelines, after 55 years of operation, were deteriorating. Internally their condition was good, but because they were originally laid down resting on timber baulks only a few inches above ground, moisture retained by the natural vegetation was causing corrosion on the underside of the pipelines. A programme was put in place to turn individual sections of both pipelines bringing the corroded areas uppermost and where necessary, welding steel plates over the corroded areas. This process meant burning out the lead in the spigoted joints prior to turning, and re-leading following turning.

This programme continued each summer for over 20 years under difficult working conditions where materials and equipment had to be moved over difficult and sensitive terrain, but the satisfaction of maintaining station operation for that period of time was ample reward.

Photo 27: Cwm Dyli's original 1905/06 pipeline viewed from the tunnel exit valve house in 1986.

A stator fault developed on No. 2 Alternator during a storm in 1971 and inspection revealed damage at more than one point. The estimated cost of repair was £800 and it was decided that this generator should remain out of service partly due to the fact that there was no reduction in the output capacity of the station.

As previously stated, electricity was originally generated to supply the industrial loads of the slate quarries, but changes over the years, including nationalisation in 1948 and the decline in the local slate industry, meant that generation took place to satisfy the needs of the wider system. This occurred generally at peak demand periods and as directed by central control, initially at Legacy substation near Wrexham, but later from the CEGB centre at Roseneath, Manchester.

Exceptions to this pattern were at times of heavy rainfall where generation took place in order to control Llyn Llydaw reservoir level.

Incidents that I can recall, or was directly involved with are as follows:

18th July 1964: 1.35 inches of rainfall at the power station in 15 minutes from 5.15 to 5.30pm.

19th February 1979: during extremely cold weather conditions, a scour valve on the "B" pipeline, at a point known as 'Wembley' on the low pressure section, fractured. The ground adjacent was scoured to a depth of 10 feet and a considerable quantity of brown water was seen coming down the Cwm Dyli Waterfall.

21st May 1980: The intermediate valve linking both pipelines immediately outside the power station building failed. Water discharged sprayed over the power station's roof.

22nd November 1980: 5¼ inches of rain in 24 hours.

27th June 1984: Station late coming on load because on operator was delayed on his journey - sheep gathering in progress on the approach track!

24th December 1984: Fire behind main switchgear from No.1 Set circuit breaker. All sets tripped and all supplies failed. Fire extinguished by station staff.

10th January 1985: Local farmer reported an overhead transmission line had come down on his land - he touched it with his 'welly boot' and received a minor burn.

Photo 28: Cwm Dyli generator control panel only slightly modified since 1906. Taken in 1985

During January and February 1986 the dam at Llyn Llydaw was demolished. This was only a small stone and concrete structure, but was nevertheless a 'dam' under the terms of the Reservoirs Act, and various consents were required before work could commence.

Studies had proved that the demolition would not affect the viable running of the station. Llyn Llydaw would revert to a natural lake and a problem concerning the overtopping of and damage by wave action to the miners causeway would be eliminated. This causeway had been constructed in about 1853 by David Prichard to facilitate the transporting of ore from the nearby copper mine.
I can vividly recall that this work was carried out by CEGB personnel in atrocious weather conditions with temperatures around -12° Centigrade.

Concurrent with the later stages of pipeline turning and plating, investigations were being undertaken regarding the long term future of the power stations at Cwm Dyli, Dolgarrog and Maentwrog. Options considered were closure, refurbishment and replanting. Major factors in the considerations were that the sites were established, rights existed and that the "fuel" was plentiful and renewable.

It was decided that Cwm Dyli should be entirely replanted and that the necessary finance should be made available. All consent and consultation procedures were undertaken and as with the original development, the Baron Hill Estate gave full backing to the replanting scheme.

Photo 29: Cwm Dyli 11kv switchgear prior to replanting

A formal shut-down ceremony took place on Monday 29th February 1988, after no less than 82 years of continuous generation from the site. At 08.30 hrs on that day, Sets 1, 3 and 4 were on load generating a total of 5MW (5,000 kW). The pre-arranged shut-down commenced at 11.00 and was complete by 11.30 hrs. The sets were taken off-load and shut-down by the following:

Set 3 - HW Golding, Station Manager Ffestiniog Group
EG Davies, Switchboard Attendant

Set 4 - CH Williams, former Superintendent Cwm Dyli
KO Evans, Turbine Driver

Set 1 - DW Thomas, Station Engineer
HE Evans, Turbine Driver

An intensive working programme for replanting commenced almost immediately. This consisted of the removal of both pipelines, all the plant within the station and the refurbishment of the joint CEGB/Manweb Substation. The original intake pipe in Llyn Llydaw was subjected to an underwater survey and was found to be in good condition, the only alteration being the provision of an anti-vortex baffle.

Pipeline replacement was to be a single steel pipe carried on saddle supports, giving sufficient ground clearance. To facilitate the removal and replacement, a single rack railway line was laid up the steepest portion of the route close to the power station, providing Cwm Dyli with its railway, 83 years after the formation of the Portmadoc, Beddgelert and South Snowdon Railway Company. Bogmats were used along the route of the low pressure section of the pipeline to protect the ground and the vegetation in a very sensitive area. These mats proved to be extremely efficient.

Some difficulties were experienced during the plant removal within the station mainly due to the quality of the original workmanship. The concrete was found to be extremely durable and the oldest machines were certainly constructed to last. The No.1 set of turbine, governor and alternator was transferred to the care of the Museum of the North at Llanberis, where perhaps one day it will be re-assembled for display purposes.

The contract for the pipeline work was undertaken by Laing Engineering, whilst the plant renewal was the responsibility of NEI Peebles. The total cost of the replanting was £5 million.

The new generating unit consists of a Francis turbine having 18 runner blades with a flowrate of 3.50 cubic metres per second, connected to an 800mm diameter penstock via a butterfly main inlet valve, all provided by Kvaerner Boving Limited, together with an NEI synchronous generator rated at 11.75 MVA. Rated speed is 1000rpm and output 10MW (compared to the previous full load 5MW). A 12.5 MVA NEI transformer operating at 11/33kW connected to the Manweb distribution system. The generator circuit breaker is a GEC manufactured vacuum circuit breaker rated at 750 MVA.

Photo 30: Cwm Dyli generating plant in 1986 - No.3 turbine nearest the camera, then No.2 Set, No.1 Set (both 1906) and No.4 (originally No.5) nearest the main door

Photo 31: The early stages of plant removal/demolition at Cwm Dyli prior to the replanting in 1988

Photo 32: Llyn Llydaw dam spillway looking from downstream, clearly showing the dry river bed. The original dam was a timber structure further upstream.

Photo 33: Llyn Llydaw dam from the upstream side.

Photo 34: January 1986 - careful manoeuvring required along the miners track leading to Llyn Llydaw prior to demolition of the dam.
Grenville Jones, catchment foreman with his back to the camera.

Photo 35: Llyn Llydaw in 1986 with demolition of the dam well advanced.

The complete replanting was carried out in a remarkably short period of time. Cwm Dyli, following initial testing and commissioning, was available for commercial operation on 10th July 1989, only 16 months after the shut-down of the previous plant.

Utilising the same quantity of the water as for the old plant, the new plant could deliver 25% more electrical units.

The new plant was designed from the start to be automatically operated and although there was initially an operator on site, it was not long before the plant was operating entirely automatically. A later change saw the site becoming completely unmanned, with remote operation from Dolgarrog. This situation constitutes a major change from the days that I remember when a Station Superintendent; Deputy Superintendent; Station Foreman; three Shift Charge Engineers; five Turbine Drivers; one Pipelinesman and one Labourer, were all employed at Cwm Dyli. A total of 13 individuals. This number was increased by wives and children, because the senior personnel were expected to live on site in bungalows erected originally by the North Wales Power Company. Indeed Cwm Dyli was a thriving small community.

Other staff would travel to work from Beddgelert, Llanberis and Blaenau Ffestiniog. I can recall as a Shift Charge Engineer, working a shift pattern of alternate evening and morning shifts on successive days. On completion of an evening shift at 11pm, having put the plant to "bed", one would proceed to follow suit and sleep in the bed provided in the staff quarters adjacent to the main building. This arrangement would sometimes become a necessity in winter, with deep snow covering the access track, even though one might be the sole occupant of the building. Arriving on time for the following days morning shift was never a problem!

Photo 36: Llyn Llydaw early in 1986, when the temperature dropped to -12°C.

Photo 37: Soon after the shutdown of Cwm Dyli for replanting in 1988, heavy rainfall resulted in an overflow from Llyn Llydaw. The spate is seen coming down the falls.

Photo 38: The same spate flowing past Cwm Dyli cottage as it would have done when the author's ancestors lived here in 1750.
The remains of the original larger house can still be seen.

Photo 39: The early stages of removal of the original Cwm Dyli pipelines in 1988.

Photo 40: Cwm Dyli new pipeline - the low pressure (upper) section.

Photo 41: Cwm Dyli new pipeline - the high pressure section with the power station in the background.

At the time of writing, electricity was first generated at Cwm Dyli 90 years ago and the new plant and pipeline will ensure that this process will be maintained for at least another 50 years, well into the next century.

c) Dolgarrog Power Station

Dolgarrog power station is situated in the village of Dolgarrog (previously the hamlet of Porthllwyd) in the Conwy valley and 6½ miles due south of Conwy.

The original development was carried out by the Aluminium Corporation Ltd, in 1907, to provide electrical power for the smelting process in the works on the same site. For the initial scheme, Llyn Eigiau was utilized for storage, the level of the natural lake being raised to 1,239 feet O.D. by means of a mass concrete gravity dam constructed in two stages between 1907 and 1911. From Eigiau, water was released to flow for about 2 miles along Afon Porthllwyd before entering a leat which led to a forebay and penstock at 1,030 feet O.D. almost immediately above the power station. The leat was later extended into the adjoining Cowlyd valley to a point on Afon Ddu with suitable intake works. A single steel pipeline, 3 feet in diameter, connected the forebay and the power station the net head being 1,006 feet. This pipeline supplied the original machines in the station, the initial equipment consisting of four 1,600 horse-power turbines coupled to continuous current generators each of 1,000kW. Afterwards, a fifth continuous current unit was installed but it was found necessary for the purpose of the aluminium works supply to replace the generator by an alternator of 1,200kW; 3 phase; 50 cycles; 1,050 volts. The original development included the building of houses by the company for their employees in the village of Dolgarrog and these properties were supplied with electricity from the power station.

The Aluminium Corporation was formed in December 1909, although some aluminium ingot had been produced at Dolgarrog in the previous year by a former company of the same name. Prior to 1914, supplies of aluminium were obtained from Germany but from the outbreak of the first World War, alumina was supplied by an associated company, International Aluminium Co. Ltd. of Northumberland which continued to supply alumina to Dolgarrog until 1944. During the 1914-18 war a small rolling mill was set up and for the first time the plant rolled its own metal - a total of 3 or 4 tons per week. After the war, rolled metal production was expanded and in a development programme, additional plant was installed and also at this time Dolgarrog village was enlarged by more than 100 houses for employees.

Following the passing of the Electricity (Supply) Act, 1919, a scheme for supplying a greater extended area was put forward by the North Wales Power Co. Ltd. which formed the subject of an enquiry held at Llandudno in 1921 by the Electricity Commissioners and resulted in an Order, dated 3 August 1923, constituting the North Wales and South Cheshire Electricity District and establishing the North Wales and South Cheshire Electricity Authority. Certain powers, rights and obligations of the Joint Authority were transferred by deed to the North Wales Power Co. which then operated under the provisions contained in the Act of 1904 and the Order of 1923 throughout the extended area of supply, covering 4,084 square miles. The technical scheme put forward by the Power Company provided for the development of the water power resources of the district and the establishment of a new hydro-electric power station at Maentwrog with an installed capacity of not less than 15,000kW.

During this period of construction, the rapidly increasing demands for electricity on the Power Company were met by purchasing power in bulk from their associated company the Aluminium Corporation Ltd. at Dolgarrog and the Mersey Power Co. Ltd. at Runcorn. The North Wales Power Company constructed a double-circuit 33kV, overhead transmission line between Percival Lane, Runcorn and their Crewe sub-station in order to supply the requirements of the London, Midland and Scottish Railway Co. for their engineering works at Crewe until such time as the supply from the new power station at Maentwrog became available.

By an agreement dated June 1923 between the Aluminium Corporation and the Power Company which is cited in the second schedule of the Order of 1923, the Corporation agreed to supply all the electricity generated at Dolgarrog as and when required by the Power Company up to a maximum demand of 10,000kW and output of 40,000 units per annum. The Corporation contracted to meet these demands by July 1925 and built an entirely new A.C. power station with an installed capacity of 10,000kW adjacent to their existing station which was put into commercial operation in that year.

However, also in 1925, progress was cut short when on Monday 2 November a failure of the Eigiau and Coedty dams occurred leading to the deaths of 10 adults and 6 children. The initial cause of the disaster was a blow-out of the lower section of a portion of the Eigiau dam wall which scoured a channel 70 feet wide and 10 feet deep below the original ground surface and the breach probably discharged somewhere in the order of 50 million cubic feet of water in the first hour of discharge, lowering the lake level by 5 feet. The water released from Eigiau surged down into the Coedty reservoir below, flooding the valley of Afon Porthllwyd in several places. Coedty reservoir, nearly full at the time, was filled to capacity within minutes, the spillway then having to cope with a surplus discharge greatly in excess of its designed capacity. In rapid sequence, the dam was overtopped in the central portion, the material supporting the wall on the downstream side was washed away and the core collapsed. Thereupon, the flood surged onwards down the valley, now compounded by the almost instantaneous release of the 70 million gallons of water from Coedty. The flood dragged large quantities of stream debris in its cascade over the lip of the hanging valley above Dolgarrog. Much of the pipework system leading to the power station was demolished and the wall of water, mud, rock and concrete hit what was Machno Terrace at the northern end of Dolgarrog village at 9.15pm. At this time, many of the villagers were attending a film show at the village Assembly Hall out of the path of the flood and had they not been, many more lives could have been lost. The flood demolished a section of the Conwy to Llanrwst road; a road bridge; several houses and cottages; a chapel and part of the water main from Cowlyd to Conwy. The aluminium factory and the power stations were encompassed by debris 6 feet deep and the factory suffered considerable damage in the flood because, as the flood waters reached the seventeen furnaces, they exploded one by one. Also, since the power station supplied electricity to the area there was a complete disruption of supply to the coastal towns nearby. The cost of repairing the damage caused a severe financial strain on the Corporation's resources.

In 1926, recovery from this set back was aided when the International Aluminium Co. supplied Dolgarrog with ingot at a favourable price through its Norwegian subsidiary A/S Haugrick Smelteverk. The dam at Eigiau was not repaired but a new spillway at a much reduced level was constructed whilst the dam at Coedty was reconstructed and the pipeline to the power station refurbished to fulfil its original intention of providing water to the turbines of the two 5,000kW 1925 machines.

The Aluminium Corporation continued to supply power in bulk to the Power Company until 1929 when as a result of the formation of the British Power and Light Corporation (1929) Ltd. the whole of the hydraulic works and the power stations at Dolgarrog were acquired by the Power Company and were then operated in conjunction with their other power stations. The catchment area for the Dolgarrog hydro-electric scheme was considerably extended by the construction of the Dulyn tunnel which conveyed water from Afon Dulyn into Llyn Eigiau and further increases in storages and catchment areas were brought about by the construction of dams at Llyn Cowlyd and Ffynnon Llugwy with a leat collecting water discharged from the Llugwy area and discharging into Llyn Cowlyd, the catchment being increased by 10,300 acres, practically all of which was over 1,200 feet O.D. level.

The contract amount for the construction of the Llugwy leat was £13,000. The Aluminium Company let the contract, Sir Douglas Fox and Partners were the Engineers, whilst Sir Robert McAlpine and Sons were the Contractors. The whole works were to be approved by Lord Penrhyn's agent. The original intention was to extract water from Llyn Idwal to the south-west of Llyn Ogwen, the water being conveyed in a wooden aqueduct across the valley floor and Telford's road (now the A5) into a leat following the ground contours to a point near the Afon Bedol, where a tunnel would be bored under Bwlch Trimarchog through to Cwm Eigiau, the water thence discharging into Llyn Eigiau. The leat as actually constructed commenced at a small intake above Glan Llugwy farm, which became a source of problems many years later, and ended to the south-west of Llyn Cowlyd, where a smaller Capel Curig leat joined, the combined flow running naturally down into Llyn Cowlyd. It is recorded that on 6th December 1922, 70 men were working on the Llugwy leat.

At this stage of the development the intention was to utilise the increased head to be obtained by connecting Eigiau and Cowlyd storage's by pipeline to the power station and for this purpose a tunnel was constructed in 1928 between Eigiau and Cowlyd, 2,000 yards in length and was of considerable importance as a means of equalising the storages by passing water from Eigiau into Cowlyd. The hydraulic service required by the AC power station brought about the development of the areas below the Cowlyd and Eigiau dams to the 876 feet O.D. level. These works consisted of modifications to Coedty dam together with leats extending in the first instance just beyond the Afon Ddu and Afon Porthllwyd. From the low level dam water was conveyed by means of a 6 feet diameter steel pipeline joining onto a 4 feet diameter high pressure pipeline connecting the turbines in the power station. With this development provision was made for extending the 4 feet diameter pipeline to Cowlyd at a later date.

Photo 42: The original penstock forebay for Dolgarrog power station at the 1000 feet OD level, showing the discharge sluices.

Figure 11

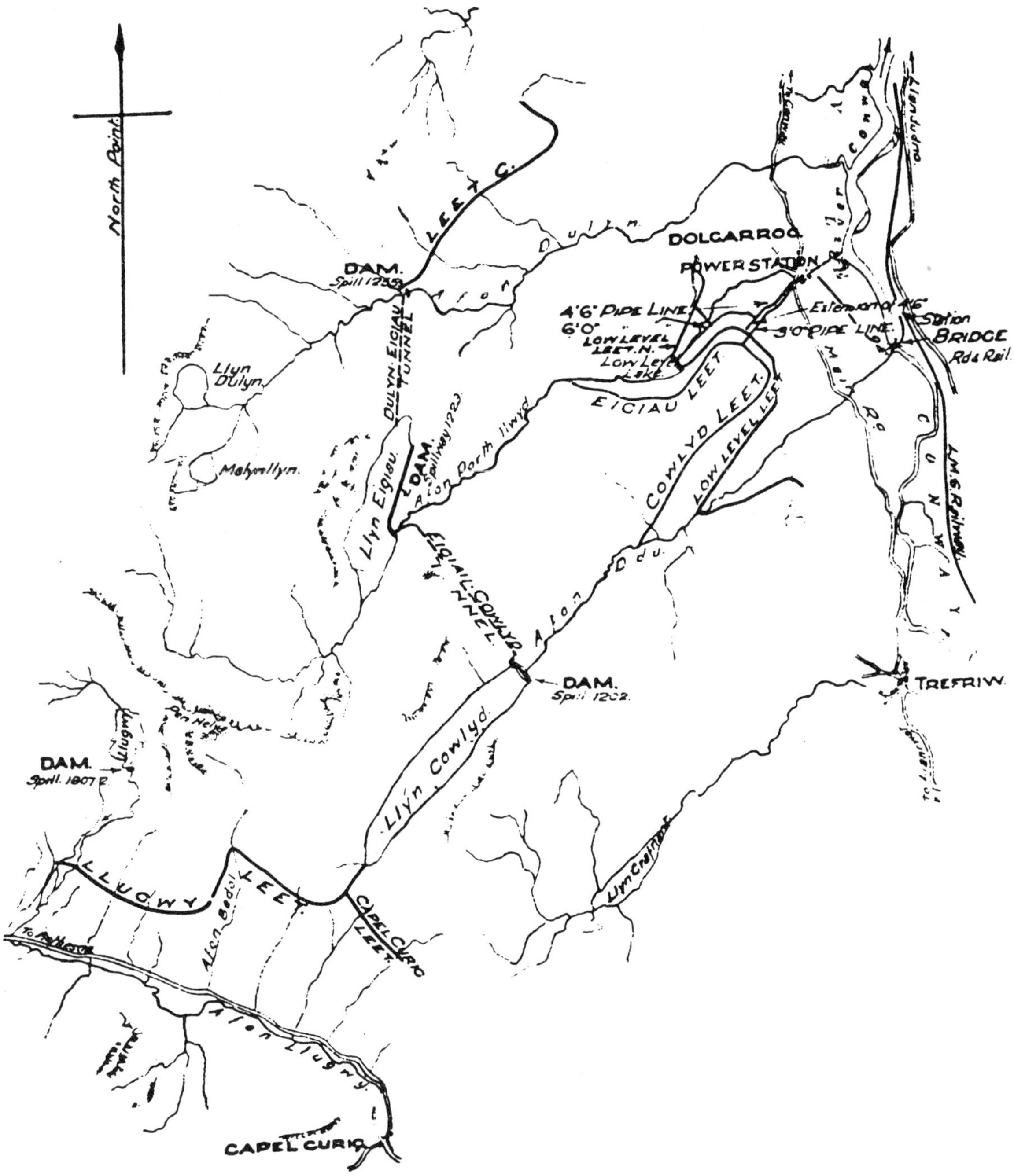

ALUMINIUM CORPORATION LTD
DOLGARROG

GENERAL PLAN OF WORKS.

SCALE 1IN TO 1MILE

DRAWING Nº D.Y.699.

In 1930, the plant installed at the power stations at Dolgarrog was as follows:

A.C. STATION

No. 1	Turbine	Alternator
Maker:	Armstrong Whitworth	English Electric Co.
Serial No:	990	WG446P
Net Head:	1100 feet	-
Output:	8300 bhp	6250kVa
Revs/min.:	428	428

No. 2		
Maker:	Armstrong Whitworth	English Electric Co.
Serial No:	991	WG447P
Net Head:	1100 feet	-
Output:	8300 bhp	6250kVa
Revs/min.:	428	428

D.C. STATION

No. 1 (Bruce Peebles)	Outer Generator	Inner Generator
Serial No:	7645	7646
KW:	500	500
Volts:	125	125
Amps:	4000	4000
Revs/min.:	450	450

No. 2 (Bruce Peebles)	Outer Generator	Inner Generator
Serial No:	7647	7648
KW:	500	500
Volts:	125	125
Amps:	4000	4000
Revs/min.:	450	450

No. 3 (Bruce Peebles)	Exciter	Alternator
Serial No:	17587	17586
KW:	28/68	1050
Volts:	-	1600
Amps:	130/260	880
No. of Poles:	4	14
Revs/min.:	428	428
Phases:	-	3
Frequency:	-	50 cycles

No. 4 (Bruce Peebles)	Outer Generator	Inner Generator
Serial No:	7651	7652
KW:	500	500
Volts:	125	125
Amps:	4000	4000
Revs/min.:	450	450

No. 5 (Bruce Peebles)	Outer Generator	Inner Generator
Serial No:	7649	7650
KW:	500	500
Volts:	40/138	40/138
Amps:	4000	4000
Revs/min.:	450	450

No. 6 Synchronous motor generator set (BTH Co. Rugby)
No. R49442 Type AKT138

Synchronous Motor	Running as Alternator
Poles: 12	KVA: 1063
KVA: 1410	Volts: 660
Volts: 6600	Amps: 93
Amps: 123.5	Revs/min.: 500
Power factor: 0.9	Frequency: 50 cycles

No. 7 Synchronous motor generator (Bruce Peebles)

Exciter	Motor	Inner Generator
No. 20492	No. 20491	No. 22777
Revs/min.: 428	KVA: 1360	KW: 540
Volts: 25/69	Volts: 6600	Volts: 130/175
Amps: 117/254	Amps: 119	Amps: 4125/3075
	Freq.: 50 cycles	

Outer Generator

No: 22778	Volts: 130/175
KW: 540	Amps: 4125/3075

No. 8 Induction motor generator (Bruce Peebles)

Induction Motor	Generator 1	Generator 2
No.: 7294	No.: 7295	No.: 7296
BHP: 850	KW: 300	KW: 300
Volts: 1050	Volts: 75	Volts: 75
Revs/min.: 365	Amps: 4000	Amps: 4000
Phases: 3	Revs/min.: 365	revs/min.: 365
50 cycles	Poles: 16	Poles: 16

No.9 Induction motor generator (Bruce Peebles)

Induction motor	Generator 1	Generator 2
No. 7291	No. 7292	No. 7293
BHP: 850	KW: 300	KW: 300
Volts: 1050	Volts: 75	Volts: 75
Revs/min.: 365	Amps: 4000	Amps: 4000
Phases: 3	Revs/min.: 365	Revs/min.: 365
50 cycles	Poles: 16	Poles: 16

No.10 Turbo-Alternator set (Bruce Peebles)

Exciter	Alternator
No. 12689	No. 12688
KW: 2.70	KAV: 187
Volts: 77	Volts: 440
Amps: 34.30	Amps: 246
Revs/min.: 1000	Poles: 6
Poles: 4	50 cycles

No. 11 Turbo generator set (Bruce Peebles)

Machine No. 8000
KW: 30
Volts: 125
Amps: 240
Revs/min.: 900
Poles: 4

D.C. Generators	Outer Generator	Inner Generator
No:	32975	32848
KW:	500	500
Full load Volts:	125	125
Amps:	4000	4000

Type MP 48/36, Form CB, 450 Revs/min.; 10 Poles

Small auxiliary booster etc.

No. B 1514	No. B 1607
DQ2: Form SD	DR6: Form SD
KW 0.36: Revs: 1300	KW: 2
Full load volts: 0.90; Amps: 4	Volts: ± 40; Amps: 50

No. 1537
DQ2: Form SD
KW: 0.0372
Volts: 110; Amps: 0.34

Photo 43: Dolgarrog's first pipeline as originally laid from the forebay to the power station. To the right is an early example of a transmission line steel tower.

Photo 44: Dam construction in progress at Llyn Eigiau in 1908.

Photo 45: Eigiau dam as completed. The "long arm" portion of the wall where the breach is now, appears to be all new concrete.

Photo 46: Eigiau dam upstream face. The final raised portion of the wall is clearly seen. The spillway has a remarkably small cross-section considering the vast expanse of this reservoir when full

Photo 47: Eigiau dam spillway after completion of the second stage of construction. Viewed from the downstream side.

In 1936, a third turbo-alternator set was installed in the A.C. station of 6,500kW capacity, comprising of a Boving, twin Pelton wheel turbine of 9,150 bhp, coupled to an English Electric alternator rated at 8,140kVa running at 600 revs/min. and in the same year the laying of a 6 feet diameter steel pipeline was commenced connecting Cowlyd reservoir to the 4 feet high pressure pipeline at level 890 feet O.D. This pipeline connected to the original outfall pipe at Cowlyd dam and there was also a 4 feet diameter branch pipe to the Eigiau-Cowlyd tunnel. In addition, provision was made for a connection to the then Conway and Colwyn Bay Joint Water Board main supply pipe for emergency usage. With the completion of this scheme, the plant at Dolgarrog operated under the full head available from Cowlyd ie. 1,150 feet whilst the areas below the Cowlyd and Eigiau reservoirs drained into the low-level reservoir at Coedty to be utilised at the 850 feet head. Cowlyd, the principal storage reservoir, had a capacity of 345,000,000 cubic feet; Eigiau was limited to 40,000,000 cubic feet and Llugwy reservoir's capacity was also 40,000,000 cubic feet.

The 1939-45 war created an enormous demand for aluminium and the output of Dolgarrog works was boosted to more than 5,000 tons per year with aircraft sheet being the dominant product but by 1944 the production of ingot had become uneconomic because of the high cost of power and imported metal from Canada had become available in quantity. The Dolgarrog smelting furnaces were thus shut down. This in turn resulted in the majority of the plant in the older station becoming redundant and as most of the machines were over 35 years old it was decided to embark on a programme of dismantling and removal. By 1946, the remaining plant consisted of a 1,200kW turbo-alternator (No.3 in the 1939 plant list) which had been commissioned in 1918 together with a D.C. generator to provide internal D.C. supplies (No.11 in the 1930 plant list). Both these machines were run off the low head system pipeline from Coedty.

Photo 48: Dolgarrog - the original power station with two turbines minus their covers either for inspection or repair..

In 1952, Parliamentary approval was obtained to extend the low-head catchment system based on Coedty reservoir and, by 1956, construction of the new Pen-y-Parc, Tafalog, Rowlyn leats, over 5 miles long, was completed which increased the area of the gathering ground by 3,400 acres and over the next two years improvements were carried out at Coedty dam, namely the provision of automatic tilting discharge gates and a new side spillway. Also in 1956, a fourth turbo-alternator was installed in the new station to run off the Coedty pipeline comprising of a Francis type horizontal turbine of 14,000 bhp, by Boving and Co. coupled to a Bruce Peebles alternator of 12,500kVa operating at a head of 810 feet and a speed of 750 revs/min. This fourth unit brought the total generating capacity of Dolgarrog power station up to 27,700kW.

Plant installed in 1957 in the 'new' station consisted of:

No.1 Set:	5000kW:	first run on 12th November, 1924
No.2 Set:	5000kW:	first run on 2nd March, 1925
No.3 Set:	6500kW:	first run on 26th September, 1936
No.4 Set:	10000kW:	first run on 12th February, 1957
No.5 Set:	1200kW:	first run in 1918

All records relating to the early period of No.5 Set were lost when the stations were flooded in 1925 but it gave many years of productive service. Following the installation of No.4 Set in 1956, No.5 Set was only used when excess water was present in Coedty reservoir and after 48 years service, it was last run on 27th June 1966 and dismantled shortly afterwards. The last remaining D.C. generator (No.11) was also taken out of service at the same time but is still in existence and can be seen in cut-away exhibition form at the Ffestiniog pumped storage station.

Photo 49: Auxiliary switchboard panel in the old DC station at Dolgarrog. Staff transport (a bicycle) is leaning on the left wall.

The mid and late 1950's was a period in which numerous improvements were carried out. In 1956/57 the original control panel for the generator and main switchgear, located on the gallery level above the turbine floor was completely removed, being replaced by a suite of panels in a newly built control room, located with its floor level 4 feet above the existing gallery level. To enable this work to proceed, a temporary control panel was situated on the turbine floor. At the same time a new outdoor substation was constructed, having a main 33kV busbar and Ferguson Pailin 33kV OCB switchgear for the generator and Manweb circuits. Previous operating voltages for generators and distribution purposes had ranged from 6.6kV to 20kV as per North Wales Power Company standards.

Previously used (for generators 1 and 2) and new (for 3 and 4) generator transformers were installed in this new substation and connections to the National Grid were via two 33/132kV transformers linked to the Connah's Quay - Treborth (Bangor) 132kV transmission line.

Photo 50: Dolgarrog AC station plant in 1937 with control panel on the gallery level.

Photo 51: Dolgarrog power station - the 1955 control room with Manweb 33kv feeders and generator control panel. Jack (Bull) Jones on the left and R Glynn Jones on the right..

Concurrently, other major work carried out was the refurbishment of Nos 1 and 2 turbines, where the original Pelton wheel runners were removed, to be replaced by runners cast from stainless steel, engineered to last for many years with minimum maintenance requirements. The turbine needle valves were also renewed in the same material, the work being carried out by Boving.

In 1959, modifications at Coedty reservoir included the removal of many tons of silt from the reservoir bed together with the construction of a new side spillway at the point where the Ardda leat entered the reservoir. This work became necessary following calculations made regarding flood studies under amendments to the 1930 Reservoirs Act, and also included the provision of automatic tilting gates, three in number, located at the original spillway near the centre of the dam. These gates opened when the weight of water against them overcame the predetermined ballast in counterweights suspended above them. The centre gate opened first to be followed on continued rise in water level by the two other gates, the water discharging in a controlled manner into the Afon Porthllwyd.

Coedty reservoir was rather volatile regarding water levels. With no inflow, the reservoir could be drawn down from maximum to minimum levels with 10MW of generation from the No.4 Set in 15 hours. Conversely at times of heavy rainfall on the extended catchment, continuous operation of No.4 Set and No.5 Set whilst it remained operational, would not abstract sufficient quantities of water to prevent spillage occurring at Coedty. At a time following the removal of the No.5 Set, I can recall No.4 Set operating continuously for a period of 7 days purely for water level control purposes.

Apart from the major incident of the dam disaster in 1925, other incidents were remarkably few and far between. Four lengths of the pipeline (4ft diameter) close to the "dead man" on the incline railway, became displaced in 1924 and caused a wash-out in the vicinity. During governor trials on No.3 Set in 1937, the venturi pipe in the penstock burst. No other damage was caused and a strengthened replacement section was fitted.

In September 1954, during the early hours of the morning, an explosion occurred, located in the 6.6kV switchgear, situated then within the station building. The building soon became full of smoke and many windows were shattered, the station yard being littered with broken glass. The ensuing fire was extinguished using portable appliances. The personnel on site at the time were the Shift Engineer RA Morris and the Turbine Driver Percy McRae.

They were both uninjured but Percy McRae's face was covered with blackened oil. The source of the explosion was located in the Llanrwst feeder cubicle. The faulty section of 6.6kV busbar was isolated in order to reinstate generating plant as the weather was particularly stormy and reservoir water levels were high.

An operational intransigence which occurred mainly at night time, if my memory serves me right, was the complete loss of all power supplies to and from the station, the substation of course acting as a major distribution point for Manweb supplies. This would happen fairly regularly at one time before the system was strengthened and would leave the site in total darkness (a later provision of emergency lighting somewhat alleviated this situation). To remedy the problem, all distribution circuit breakers, both 11kV and 33kV, were opened and either No.5 Set would have to be run up, which was never easy in the dark, to energise the 11kV busbars, or No.3 Set which had a hand operated bearing oil system pump, was run up to energise the 33kV busbars. Selected distribution feeders could then be restored to provide load and station supplies. Being on duty during this type of event called for methodical thinking, staff co-operation and a functional hand lamp!

One incident which proved to be stressful for many people was when a potential land slip was discovered above a row of houses in Dolgarrog village. Some earth movement was observed and it was thought to be linked to the presence of the Ardda leat close to the ridge on the hillside above the village. Residents were evacuated and temporarily housed in purpose built units close to the aluminium factory. Investigations were carried out which disproved any link with excess water from the leat and eventually normality returned.

The station was continuously manned 24 hours per day, seven days a week, by staff who took pride in their work. The complement normally consisted for many years of a Station Superintendent and his Deputy, both of whom lived locally in company owned properties; four Shift Charge Engineers; four Turbine Drivers; one Mechanical Fitter; one fitter's mate and also a Catchment Foreman; a (Pipe)linesman; two locomotive drivers for the Cowlyd Tramway; a Storeman; a vehicle driver together with twelve catchment labourers. Certain individuals stand out in the memory and in quieter moments one could be entertained "in-house" by a carnival marshal in full regalia or have a haircut done by an individual who was himself as "bald as a coot". This same individual was also somewhat prone to sickness and he would be regularly goaded that the only ailment he did not encounter was dandruff. Percy McRae, already mentioned earlier, a gentleman by nature, would cycle to and from work and if he arrived at the station six or seven minutes before the shift start time, he would cycle around the station yard until precisely two minutes were in hand before entering the building. Happy days!

Reverting to engineering matters, increasing plant operating and staff costs resulted in the removal of the Shift Charge Engineers' posts and the creation of Switchboard Attendants positions. Another innovation was the as then termed "automation" of the No.4 Set, using Ferranti SC900 sequence control equipment, designed to operate the machine from standstill to full load and in the reverse order, either by manual operation of a single switch, or on rising/falling reservoir level, or for a predetermined clock time.

Many expensive hours were used to install switches, relays, control panels and cabling, but it is not surprising, on reflection, that a system originally conceived for use in a biscuit factory was not entirely suited to the control of hydro turbine-generators. Satisfactory operation was brief and manual intervention was necessary for the functions of synchronising, loading and unloading.

The dams and reservoirs were, under the conditions laid down in the 1930 Reservoirs Act and the later Act of 1975, continuously monitored and regularly inspected. From time to time some defects became apparent and work over and above the normal maintenance works became necessary. The following can be noted for the associated reservoirs:

Eigiau

1926: Spillway lowered by 12 feet

1929: Spillway lowered by 4 feet

1989: Discontinuance as a reservoir following many years of continued deterioration of the original concrete dam wall. The spillway was completely removed and a concrete pipeline laid underground from a new intake works in the lake, to connect directly into the existing Eigiau-Cowlyd tunnel. From 19th July 1989, Eigiau reverted to a natural lake but still had the capability of transferring any inflowing water through to Cowlyd.

Cowlyd

1926: Top water level reduced marginally and a wave wall constructed along the top of the dam.

1930: Spillway crest level reduced.

1963: Upstream slope repaired by concreting and stone pitching.

1974: Additional rock-fill placed on downstream slope.

Coedty

The works in 1959 have been noted earlier. These were followed by:

1972: Remedial work to core wall by deep grouting.

1987: November - Centre tilting gate secured in the lowered position, effectively reducing storage capacity prior to remedial works.

1989 June - Reservoir de-watered completely for comencement of major refurbishment undertaken be Balfour Beatty comprising of de-silting; strengthening of the upstream and downstream embankments by the depositionj of additional bulk material; installation if a new isolating valve at the intake and the fitting of a GRP lining in the drew-off tunnel.

The foregoing demonstrate the commitment to maintain these important structures in a first class condition.

Photo 52: Dolgarrog turbine hall in 1958. Set 1 in the foreground, then 2, 3, and 4.

In June 1991 the No. 4 Set was the subject of uprating modifications concentrated mainly on the turbine, its associated shaft seal and relief valve operating system. For many years following the removal of the No. 5 Set and the additional 1MW capability it provided, which was extremely useful at times of high water inflow, the No.4 machine was run for limited periods at up to 11MW as distinct from its normal 10MW loading. The uprating would allow this unit to produce 12MW continuously when required. The modification proved to be extremely successful, the capital outlay incurred being recouped within 12 months.

The main pipelines, both High Head from Cowlyd and Low Head from Coedty as a matter of routine, were inspected regularly, both externally and internally. The original coatings were a red-lead base with a hot-applied bituminous over coating. Over the years various alternative paints had been applied in order to maintain the steel in good condition and these were mainly successful with the proviso that the treatment lasted for only a few years, which entailed a recurring painting programme. In 1990 an intensive refurbishment process was commenced whereby the existing coatings were removed by grit blasting down to bare metal followed by the application of a modern two-part epoxy coating both internally and externally. Within the following 2 years, both pipelines were completely treated using this method and no further treatment will be necessary for up to 20 years. An in-built bonus was the reduction of friction losses provided by the new coating resulting in more efficient water transfer, thus increasing the overall productivity of the station.

On the High Head pipeline, the passage of time had resulted in some corrosion under and adjacent to a proportion of the pipeline support saddles, which constituted of a concrete base with a steel saddle plate mounted on a support bearing. To alleviate this problem, the pipeline had to be supported whilst each saddle and base was removed to be replaced by a PTFE impregnated contact plate and a new concrete base. This work involving numerous saddles was undertaken with the pipeline in operation and full of water. The new saddles and new coatings resulted in a pipeline which was in effect better than new.

The evaluation studies regarding the hydro stations, already mentioned in relation to Cwm Dyli, had to take into account the condition of the existing plant. The turbines at Dolgarrog were in good order, but the governors were showing their age and the alternators, not having had any major attention throughout their long existence, were in a condition such that a failure could occur at any time. Nos.1, 2 and 3 Alternators had brittle insulation and suspect windings, (No.4 Alternator was not as old and had been removed for refurbishment in 1989). Other important considerations were that the renewable water resources were available and that the large catchment areas contained major engineering structures including dams, pipelines and leats, capable of sustaining generation for a considerable period of time well into the future.

Reasoned argument bore fruit and budgetary provisions were sanctioned for the replanting of the High Head plant within the station. This did not include any work outside the confines of the station site but did include new penstock pipework and modifications to the water discharge tailrace tunnels. The work required the total shutdown of the associated plant and beforehand, the reservoir level at Cowlyd was drawn down to its minimum operating level. Since Cowlyd was always a joint-use reservoir, this meant that a considerable quantity of water remained in the reservoir for the use of Welsh Water.

The existing plant was last run as follows:

No.1 Set:	9th March 1992	after 67 years service
No.2 Set:	14th March 1992	after 67 years service
No.3 Set:	14th March 1992	after 55 years service.

(Operators on duty at the closing ceremony were: Les Roberts, Jim Atkinson, Roy Moores and Mike Hughes). Final operation was for the purpose of dewatering the pipeline.

Work began apace to dismantle and remove for scrap the associated penstock pipework, the turbines, generators, generator transformers and high voltage switchgear. Civil engineering works were undertaken to accommodate the new plant, which comprised two units replacing the previous three being orientated at an angle of 90° difference to the previous layout.

The new Francis turbines were of Weir Pumps Ltd manufacture rated at 10MW each with an individual flow rate of 3.69 m^3/second, running at 1000 rpm and having an efficiency of 92.54%. The penstock pipework and associated isolating valves were of 900mm diameter and were connected only to the High Head pipeline, there being no intermediate cross-over connection to the Low Head system as in the past.

Photo 53: Dolgarrog - the early stages of High-head replanting.

Photo 54: Dolgarrog - the new Nos 2 and 3 Sets after replanting.

The generators were constructed by GEC being of 13MVA at 11kV with an efficiency of 96%. New generator transformers and circuit breakers were also provided by GEC to connect onto the Manweb 33kV system.

The 1956 vintage control panel in the control room was to become redundant as far as the generating plant was concerned, because a new control desk was required to give manual control of the new plant designated Nos. 2 and 3 Sets, whilst including the Cwm Dyli Unit as No.1 Set with the remaining Dolgarrog machine retaining its designation as No.4 also being included. The old control panel was retained for control of the Manweb 33kV feeders.

Control of all generators was provided by a SCADA (Supervision Control And Data Acquisition) computerised system capable of pre-programmed non-attended operation, including instigation of generation on rate of rise of reservoir level. Full mimic presentation of all plant functions were provided in a display monitor located on the control desk, whilst an identical system was provided in the new administration building.

This "state of the art" operating system contrasted sharply from previously employed methods. The writer remembers well from his days as a 23 year old Shift Charge Engineer at Dolgarrog, the procedure for running up and synchronising the old No.5 Set onto the system. The set itself was of course situated in the old DC station building whilst the control panel was in the control room of the present station. The turbine driver would carry out the necessary actions to run the machine up to synchronous speed and engage the governor. Once conditions were stable the turbine driver would contact the control room by telephone and leave the line open, since once the excitation had been raised and the synchroscope activated, it would be necessary to adjust the speed of the set. Making oneself heard was not an easy task because the set, with its large open flywheel and semi enclosed alternator located in a cavern of a building, produced quite a noise. Directions would be given of the "up a touch" or "down a shade" variety until the circuit breaker was closed and loading commenced.

The method used to bring this set to a standstill defies description!

The new Nos. 2 and 3 Sets became available for commercial operation in November 1992, 58 years to the month from the first running of the original No.1 Set.

Another portion of the engineering "jig-saw" was the scheme to provide another new turbine-generator to fully utilise the capabilities of the Low Head pipeline. This set was designated No.5 and the contract for its supply and erection went to Gilbert Gilkes and Gordon of Kendal, a company which under slightly differing titles has appeared more than once during this work.

A new additional building was erected as a sideways extension of the power station building to accommodate a Francis turbine and a GEC alternator operating at 1000 rpm, whilst an associated transformer of Brush manufacture, being of 6.25 MVA was sited in the substation. This unit, capable of operating on the High or Low Head systems, was rated at 5MW and commenced commercial operation on 1st August 1994.

In 1995, the 33kV substation was completely refurbished when all the Manweb feeder circuit breakers and associated equipment were renewed. With the exception of No.4 turbine, alternator and generator transformer, Dolgarrog is now virtually a new hydro-electric power station, capable of remaining in operation for another 60 years at least. A remarkable concept especially when considering that 1997 will see 90 years of electricity generation from the site.

d) Maentwrog Power Station

A scheme, promoted by the North Wales Power Company, to augment the power output from their system by constructing a hydro-electric station at Maentwrog was submitted for approval to the Electricity Commissioner at a public enquiry in 1921. The initial phase of the development commenced in 1925 and was completed in 1928.

The Maentwrog hydro-electric scheme was situated in the valley of the Afon Prysor which joins the Afon Dwyryd near the village of Maentwrog. An artificial reservoir was formed close to the village of Trawsfynydd at a location known originally as Pandy'rddwyryd, by the construction of four concrete dams. The principal dam across the Afon Prysor, known as the "main dam", was the first major concrete arch dam to be constructed in this country and its dimensions were, 96 feet above ground level; 37 feet base width with a spillway level of 650 feet O.D. The maximum static head was 630 feet. The other three dams were of mass construction, gravity type, without spillways, serving as "cut-off" dams.

Photo 55: Maentwrog power station prior to replanting with three out of the four units in view.

The water for the initial development derived from a catchment area varying in altitude from 650 to 2800 feet O.D. and extending to 23 square miles, the run-off draining naturally into the lake via the Afon Prysor. The catchment area was for the most part steeply sloping and rocky and in view of the heavy rainfall and its practically continuous distribution throughout the year, a high percentage run-off could be obtained, the whole catchment area feeding by direct and natural channels to the reservoir. The precipitation was from 70 to 110 inches per annum and reservoir capacity 1,200 million cubic feet.

Water from the reservoir entered the pressure system through a screening chamber and thence into a 30 foot length of 10 feet diameter steel pipe between the outlet and the No.1 tunnel. At the point of entry into the tunnel an 8ft 6 inch automatic self closing butterfly valve was fitted as protection against a burst on the low pressure pipeline. The tunnel was driven through rock and lined with concrete being of 10 feet internal diameter and 1920 feet in length. An air shaft was positioned near the entrance of the tunnel and carried to a level above the main dam. The low pressure conduit between the No.1 and No.2 tunnels comprised of 5700 feet of 9 feet 6 inches diameter riveted steel pipeline with manholes, scour valves and air valves in suitable positions. The No. 2 tunnel, situated between the low-pressure conduit and the high-pressure pipeline was of 10 feet in diameter, similar in construction to the No. 1 tunnel but with a length of 1500 feet. a surge tower, 20 feet in diameter, was constructed at the highest point of the tunnel and was formed by excavating a vertical shaft and, because of the nature of the ground over the tunnel, only 13 feet of the surge tower is above ground.

The high-pressure pipeline was constructed of lap-welded steel pipe of 73½ inch outside diameter having parallel bump joints, single or double riveted. Concrete anchor blocks were placed at each position where the slope changed and intermediate concrete piers were provided at intervals, an expansion joint being provided immediately downstream of each anchor block and at the outlet of No. 2 tunnel.

In 1934, additional plant was installed in the form of a fourth turbo-alternator similar to the existing three, having an output of 6000kW and bringing the total installed capacity up to 24,000kW. A second high-pressure pipeline was also laid down from the existing spare isolating valve at the No. 2 tunnel outlet down to the power house where an intermediate valve was fitted to enable the two high pressure pipelines to be coupled together.

Of some interest is the fact that Maentwrog was the only one of the North Wales hydro stations to be camouflage painted during the second World War even though it was the least conspicuous station because, before construction commenced, the landowner, Mrs Inge, of Plas Tan-y-Bwlch, a descendant of the Oakeley family, had insisted that trees should be planted around the site so that the power station would not be visible from her home.

In the Act of 1952, as approved by Parliament, an increase in the catchment area to Trawsfynydd reservoir was carried out and some 7 miles of aqueducts comprising open box and pipe construction were laid down enabling the station output to be increased to 53 million units per annum. The addition to the catchment area extended to some 14 square miles on the southern side of Trawsfynydd lake.

Initial operation of the Maentwrog turbo-alternators was as follows:

No. 1 Set	first run on 4th April 1928 for bearing test
No. 2 Set	first run on 29th April 1928 for bearing test
No. 3 Set	first run on 16th May 1928 for bearing test
No. 4 Set	first run on 11th October 1934 for bearing test

No. 2 Set	first generated on 18th June 1928 for 2.2 hrs producing 2,300 kWh.
No. 1 Set	first generated on 19th June 1928 for 7.25 hrs producing 8,500 kWh.
No. 3 Set	first generated on 2nd July 1928 for 3.55 hrs producing 4,640 kWh.

Photo 56: A visit to Maentwrog power station in 1948 by officers of the B.E.A., with Mr R Coupe the Station Superintendent explaining a point to Lord Citrine whilst W Jones, the turbine driver rests his hand on the governor pipework.

The CEGB received the Minister of Power's consent for the construction of Trawsfynydd nuclear power station in July 1958 and work was started in Trawsfynydd reservoir in connection with the new station's cooling water system soon after. A total of 35 million gallons per hour were required and water was to be drawn from the north end of the lake near to the main dam and returned on the south end by specially constructed channels and embankments. Since 1958 therefore, the Trawsfynydd reservoir supplied the joint requirements of the Maentwrog and Trawsfynydd power stations.

During the period of construction work at the nuclear power station and the associated works in the reservoir, Maentwrog power station was called upon to regulate reservoir levels, the object being to maintain low water levels. On 14th November 1959, the station was operating under extreme conditions at an abnormally low reservoir level of 619 feet OD with 3 generators on load to prevent a rise in water level. Surge action on the water flow between the intake screens in the reservoir and the automatic self closing valve situated some 30 feet down stream of the dam, caused vibration of the valve actuating paddle. This resulted in closure of the valve and with generation continuing, all the water in the pipeline and tunnels was drawn off through the turbines. The only indication of abnormality at the station was the loss of load on the generators and the decrease in pipeline pressure. The generators were off loaded and brought to rest without mishap but an inspection of the low pressure section of the pipeline revealed that it had collapsed into a horseshoe shape. Investigations found that the existing anti-vacuum valves were of insufficient capacity to have prevented this failure and during the reconstruction of the pipeline, this deficiency was rectified. I was involved with the monitoring and observations during the initial refilling and recommissioning of the pipeline in 1962.

Following the commissioning of Trawsfynydd power station, Maentwrog was restricted regarding reservoir usage, the top 5 feet of water only being available for hydro generation purposes.

The automation previously mentioned in relation to Dolgarrog No.4 Set was also undertaken in 1977 at Maentwrog, but here, all four units were modified. equipment was installed to automatically operate all the auxiliary hydraulic valves together with the main inlet valves. The governors were arranged to be continuously engaged with electric motors fitted to drive oil pumps to maintain governor pressure as distinct from the previous arrangement whereby the pumps were belt driven from the turbine shaft. Automatic start-up and shut-down took place via interposing relays acting to drive the governor speeder motors. There was automatic alternator excitation, synchronising and loading with reverse actions for the unloading and shut-down sequence. New control panels were installed adjoining the existing control panel situated on the gallery level above the turbine floor, no separate control room as at Dolgarrog ever existed at Maentwrog.

The whole scheme was based on the Ferranti SC900 sequence control equipment and was not to be an outstanding success. In retrospect, the fitting of modern control equipment onto elderly machinery was not the best course of action. Although reductions in staff numbers were achieved, operation of the plant necessitated manual intervention and during periods of extended plant operation, continuous manning was required.

Also around this time, it became apparent that the turbine runner buckets were subject to metal fatigue. The cast steel buckets had numerous cracks mainly in the dished sections. A regular procedure was established during overhaul periods, whereby inspections were undertaken to include dye penetrant and magnetic particle tests of the buckets to pinpoint the cracked areas. These cracks were monitored and where necessary repairs were carried out either by metal stitching or welding.

In common with Cwm Dyli and Dolgarrog, the plant at Maentwrog was well maintained and continued to give satisfactory service although plant assessments were ongoing in 1981 and highlighted several areas that would require attention in the near future, including the insulation of the alternator stators.

The main dam constructed across the Afon Prysor having been commenced in 1924, had been subject to remedial works in the ensuing years. In 1931, pressure grouting was carried out at the main dam and the Gyfywys cut-off dam, whilst in 1934/35, the upstream face of the main dam had a new outer skin applied. However, in 1986, it was discovered that the concrete of the main dam was subject to alkali-silica reaction or "concrete cancer". Deliberations regarding remedial action took a relatively short time and influenced to a certain extent by the continuing presence of Trawsfynydd power station and its requirements of 34 million gallons of reservoir water per hour, the decision was made to construct a new replacement dam.

Preliminary work began in April 1987 and the construction of the new dam commenced in 1988, 75 metres downstream of the original main dam. Keirs were the main contractors for the scheme, whilst Boving were responsible for the mechanical aspects in relation to intake works and pipeline connection to the existing arrangements. Excavation of the foundations took over a year followed by the pouring of 54,500 cubic metres of concrete in 19 blocks to form an "S" shaped gravity dam 219 metres long rising 38.8 metres above its foundations to a crest level of almost 200 metres OD (656 feet). The area between the old and new dams was then flooded before the top of the old dam was removed. This major work was completed in December 1991. Official opening took place on 29 February 1992 and the cost incurred was £10 million.

Reverting to 1986, a major incident occurred in March of that year, when a pipeline and valve failure at the high pressure section at Penyfoel, which is at the top of the slope above the power station, sent water cascading down the hillside. Trees were uprooted, soil and scree were washed away in the path of the flood and as a result, the A496 Maentwrog to Harlech road was completely blocked. A house situated to the rear of the station building was also in the path of the debris and suffered considerable damage. Fortunately there were no personal injuries but as a consequence the power station, obviously, was non-operational.

Repairs were authorised and because other factors such as the previously mentioned plant assessments together with the ongoing construction of the new dam, it was determined that the station at Maentwrog would be replanted.

The existing plant was finally shut-down in April 1991. The four machines were totally removed to be replaced by two new units each capable of generating 15MW bringing the stations capacity up to 30MW as compared to the previous 24MW. The Francis reaction turbines, comprising of 17 blade runners having a diameter of 1120mm, operating at the existing head of 183 metres, turn at 600rpm. the 17.65 MVA salient, 10 pole, brushless exciter alternators generate at 11,000Volts and are linked to generator transformers which increase the voltage to 33,000 Volts. This is the voltage at which the main Manweb distribution system operates, local distribution being at 11,000 Volts. A further transformer connects Maentwrog into the 132kV network and the National Grid system.

The new turbines were provided by Kvaerner Boving whilst the alternators were of GEC Alsthom manufacture. Automatic control was via a GEC Gem 80 system.

Coincidental with these major works was the pipeline refurbishment where the original paint was removed down to base metal, which was then coated with an epoxy product.

Full load water flow for the new plant stands at 14,810 litres per second. The old plant at 24MW consumed 11,837 litres per second whilst the corresponding figure for the new 30MW is 12,346. The first of the new machines turned initially on 30th November 1991 followed by the second machine on 24th December 1991.

The station was officially re-opened in February 1992, the cost of the replanting having totalled £4 million.

Full automatic, remote capable operation commenced in 1994 and all the foregoing work will ensure an extended life of at least 60 years. Trawsfynydd power station reached the end of its operational life in 1993, but its near neighbour at Maentwrog having commenced operating in 1928, has already been in service for 68 years, and will continue to generate electricity in an environmentally friendly manner for many more years.

It has been my privilege to be involved in the operation of Dolwen power station during my period of service at Ffestiniog power station in 1961/62 and to have been based at different times at Cwm Dyli, Maentwrog and Dolgarrog power stations respectively. My first acquaintance with Maentwrog power station occurred in 1958 whilst still serving my apprenticeship. It has also been my pleasure to have worked with countless numbers of staff who always took a pride in their work whatever the task.

Photo 57: Maentwrog power station exterior in 1995 showing the high pressure pipelines and penstocks.

Photo 58: Trawsfynydd reservoir and the new main dam (1995).

Photo 59: Maentwrog turbine hall following the replanting.

Photo 60: Maentwrog power station main generator control panel still displaying its South Wales Switchgear maker's plate and the original frequency meter.

3.4 Schemes where Electricity was not the Prime Objective

The major scheme in this category is located at Llyn Celyn on the Afon Tryweryn some 4 miles north-west of Bala and some 6 miles in a direct line from Richard Edwards' base at Llanuwchllyn.

Llyn Celyn is operated in conjunction with Llyn Tegid (Bala) and Llyn Brenig to control the flows into the River Dee to ensure a supply of water to abstractors and to alleviate floods. The National Rivers Authority have a major controlling influence relating to water levels in the reservoir and water flows in the river. International canoeing events are held on the Afon Tryweryn downstream of Llyn Celyn.

Construction of the reservoir was authorised by the Liverpool Corporation Act 1957 to impound the water of the Afon Tryweryn. The scheme was to provide 295,000 ml/day of water for the then Liverpool Corporation to abstract at their waterworks at Huntington on the River Dee. Construction began on 2nd August 1960, the first filling of Llyn Celyn beginning on 1st September 1964, whilst it was inaugurated on 21st October 1965 and finally completed in early 1966 at a cost of approximately £3 million.

The catchment area of the reservoir rises to 2900 feet above ordnance datum at Arenig Fawr and is mainly moorland. Run-off from the subsidiary catchment of the Afon Hesgin is led into the reservoir by a piped catchwater. The average annual rainfall over the whole area is about 77 inches whilst on Arenig Fawr it is over 90 inches with 60 inches at the dam.

The earth dam rises 147 feet above the stream bed and is 2200 feet long on the crest forming a reservoir of 17,800 million gallons gross capacity, 816 acres in surface area. The reservoir length is 2½ miles and its maximum width is 1 mile.

Reservoir water passes through a draw-off tower of unusual design in that it is a siphon controlled multi-level draw-off. Abstraction is made via one or more of the five compressed air controlled siphon inlets spaced at 20 feet vertical centres in the tower. Each siphon can pass a maximum flow of 250 million gallons per day. The siphon system reduces the need for valves and pipework in the tower, but the tower, with its siphons can, if necessary be de-watered by sealing plates fitted on the outside face of the intakes, an exercise which necessitates a diving operation. Flow through the tower can be shut off by breaking the siphons and either by lowering a bulkhead and gate in the tower wet well or by closing the automatic self-closing valve in the draw-off pipeline in the base. The tower also incorporates a separate 18 inch emergency inlet for the discharge of compensating water if the main system should be out of service.

Figure 12: - Llyn Celyn Draw-off Tower

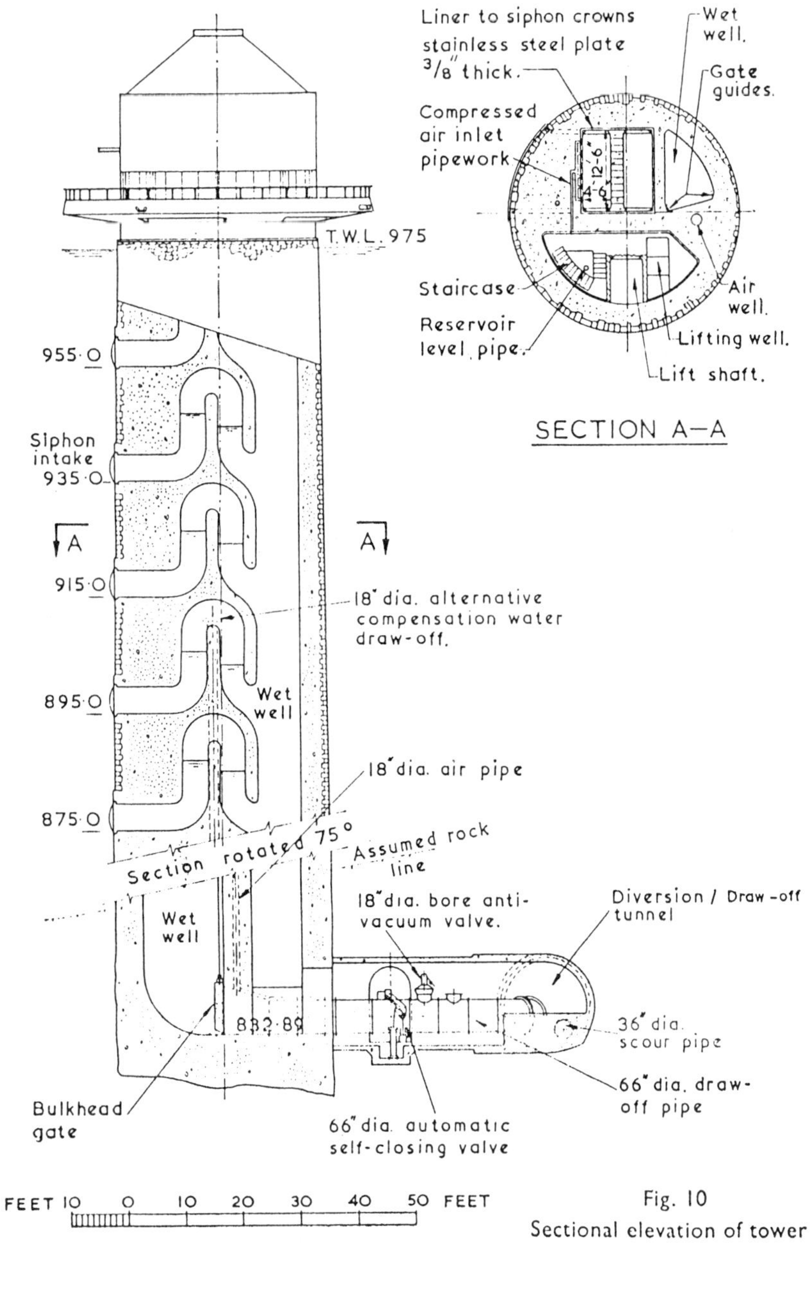

Fig. 10
Sectional elevation of tower

Photo 61: Llyn Celyn - aerial view of the dam.

Photo 62: Llyn Celyn reservoir and draw-off tower.

Although the prime objective of the scheme did not include generation of electricity, the fact that constant water discharges would be occurring meant that the addition of a purpose built power station would be extremely beneficial in providing additional income from the scheme. The power station building was therefore incorporated in the headworks.

At the downstream end of the draw-off tunnel, the 66 inch pipeline bifurcates so as to supply both the power station turbine and the discharge regulators. Through either of the 52 inch dispenser valves is discharged the normal maximum abstraction of 250 mgd at an operating head of 50 feet if the turbines are non-operational for any reason. The regulators discharge via steel lined tubes which permit full aeration of the discharged water whilst also limiting the spread of the jet. Cross connections, 18 inches in diameter, at both ends of the tunnel enable limited amounts of water to be passed through the regulators or the turbines. Sudden pipeline failure is safeguarded against by the incorporation of the water velocity initiated 66 inch butterfly valve.

The power station building, a light and airy structure clad with masonry incorporates the incoming pipework; turbines; generators; tailraces; storage and workshop facilities; high voltage switchgear; operational control centre of the reservoir and power plant.

The operation of the power station is substantially determined by the need to regulate river water flows both in the Afon Tryweryn and via the Bala sluices in the River Dee. The generating plant was therefore designed to be capable of efficient operation over the whole range of flows (7 to 250 MGD) and for a significant range of heads. The four hydro-electric sets installed have respective ratings of 2.82, 1.15, 0.43 and 0.10 MW, the largest sets generating electricity for export purposes whilst the 0.10 MW set is used to provide auxiliary headworks supplies only.
Further plant details are tabulated below:

No:	**1**	**2**	**3**	**4**
Turbine:				
Maker	Gilkes	Gilkes	Gilkes	Gilkes
Type	Francis	Francis	Francis	Turgo
Speed rpm	432	604	1012	1500
Generator:				
Maker	Brush	Brush	Brush	Brush
Type	Induction	Induction	Induction	Statically excited alternator
Volts	11,000	11,000	415	415
Amps	170	75	647	-

Hydraulic power packs control the operation of the auxiliary valves, the main inlet valves and the turbine guide vanes.

Photo 63: Llyn Celyn power station exterior.

Photo 64: Llyn Celyn discharge outlets and basin.

The original high voltage switchgear consisted of Brush oil circuit breakers (OCB) which has since been replaced with Whippe and Bourne Vacuum circuit breakers (VCB), still located within the power station building.

Outgoing generation is fed via an underground cable linking into the Manweb substation situated ¼ mile away on the north side of the valley. This substation forms part of the Maentwrog Power Station to Rhostyllen (Wrexham) 33kV transmission line.

The high voltage arrangement is shown on the folowing sketch:

Figure 13:

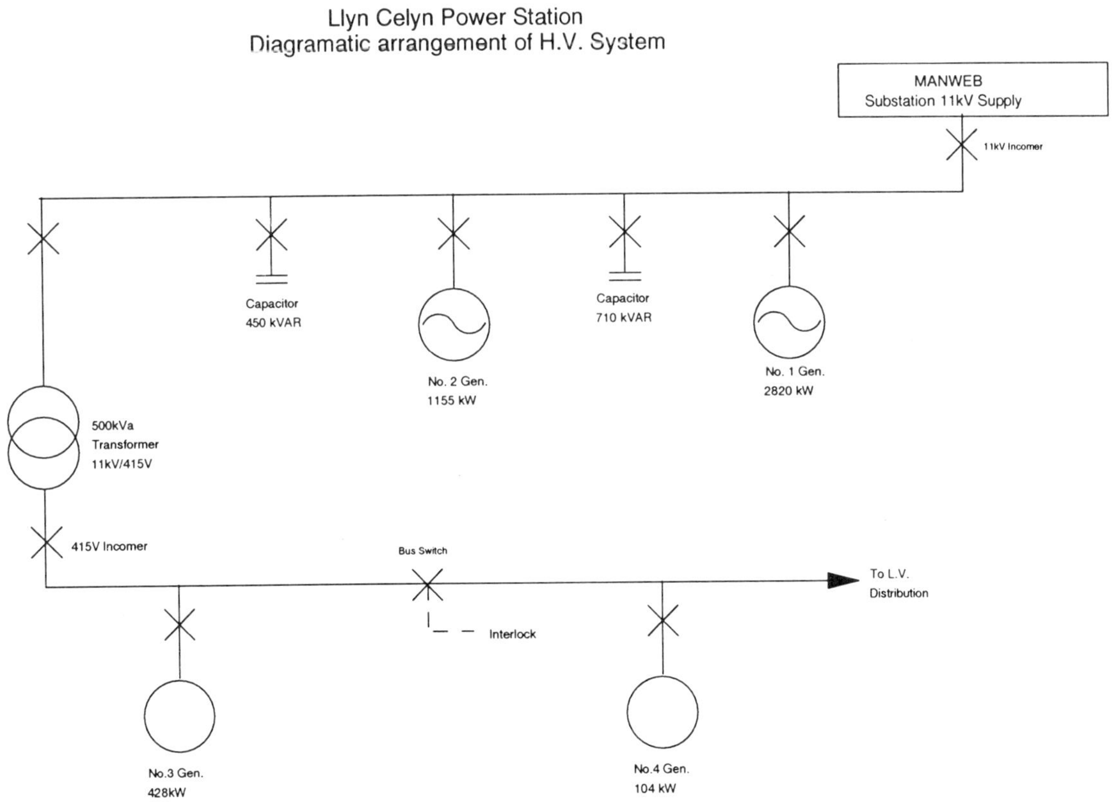

The maximum 4MW of generation occurs at the higher reservoir levels, the load decreasing as water level reduces. The rate of water discharge can vary widely to regulate the flow in the River Dee and the consequential amount of electricity generated from time to time is also variable, which is admirably catered for by the differing outputs of the four sets. Another factor which affects output is the slow process of peat build up in the draw-off system, causing a loss in water transfer efficiency. This peat is periodically cleaned away.

The power station also houses the control and metering equipment for the discharge of water from the reservoir.

Photo 65: Afon Tryweryn measuring wier.

Photo 66: Llyn Celyn draw-off tunnel under the dam and the 66 inch pipeline.

Photo 67: Llyn Celyn power station interior with No.1 Set nearest the camera.

Photo 68: Llyn Celyn power station with No.4 Set in the foreground.

When generating commenced in 1965, the power station was fully staffed, being manned 24 hours per day, 7 days per week. This is not the current situation, shifts being worked in accordance with requirements. Another recent innovation has been the installation of new control equipment and a computer based system for local automatic operation of the hydro-electric plant.

Financial returns for electricity sales are based on the NFFO (Non Fossil Fuel Obligation) which is a contractual system set up nationally to encourage non-fossil, renewable sources of generation. Remuneration is based on a predetermined price per unit if and when generation occurs and is entirely separate from the pool system.

The Llyn Celyn installation is impressive in its conception and standard of maintenance. Some of the foregoing information has been derived from a paper by HH Crann PhD, BSc, M.I.C.E., kindly provided by Fred Cook of Dwr Cymru. I am also indebted to Alun Jones who provided me with an informative grand tour at Celyn.

Chapter 4

THE NORTH WALES POWER COMPANY LIMITED

This company as originally conceived, produced all of its electrical power from hydro-electric sources and eventually embraced the power stations at Cwm Dyli and Maentwrog, which it constructed, together with Dolgarrog, which it acquired.

On 2nd May 1900 the North Wales and District Light Railway and Electric Power Syndicate Limited, was registered. The syndicate was formed to carry on the business of an electric traction and power company in all its branches; to construct, establish and maintain all necessary lines etc, electrical and mechanical engineering. A Light Railway Order applied for in November 1900, was approved authorising the construction of a linc between Pwllheli, Ncvin and Porthdinllaen. This Order was withdrawn and another application made in May 1903, for a junction with the Cambrian Railways at Pwllheli and to include a line 11 mile in length with a gauge of 4 feet 8½ inches.

The Syndicate was superseded by the North Wales Power and Traction Company Limited, which was registered on 30th July 1903. The Company intended to carry on the business of electricians, electrical, mechanical and general engineers; suppliers of light, heat and power by electricity; owners of tramways, railways and other means of transport. Authorised capital was £270,000 comprised of 54,000 shares at £5 each. A Light Railway Order, applied for in November 1903, was approved, having a route length of 13¼ miles and a gauge of 1 foot 11½ inches.

The minutes of an Extraordinary General Meeting of the Company held on Friday 22nd January 1904, at St Helens Place, London, at which Joseph Beecham was in the chair, records that the Light railway referred to was from "South Snowdon" to "Betws-y-Coed".

At a meeting of the Company's directors held on 29th September 1903, it was noted that surveys had taken place of the "railway as far as Capel Curig and the new proposed line from Corwen to Bangor".

In a further meeting on 22nd October 1903, it was revealed that "....£10,000 purchase money of the Croesor Railway had been paid into the Bank of England and that the Croesor Railway therefore belongs to this Company......"

Also, in 1904, by the North Wales Electric Power Act, the undertaking of the Portmadoc, Beddgelert and South Snowdon Railway Act, 1901, was transferred to the Company. This Act also authorised the supply of electricity within the Counties of Caernarvon, Denbigh (exclusive of the Borough of Wrexham and Wrexham Rural District), Merioneth and Anglesey. It was under the terms of this Act that the power station at Cwm Dyli was constructed in 1905/06.

The first Annual General Meeting of the Company was held on Friday 9th December 1904, at the Company's offices, 13 St Helens Place, London. The board of directors were:

James Ernest Rawlings; Syston Court near Bristol
Joseph Beecham; St Helens, Lancashire
James Tomkinson; Willington Hall, Tarporley, Cheshire
Col. Henry Platt, CB; Gorddinog, Llanfairfechan
Alfred Deedes; Frenchay Manor near Bristol
HR Hogg; 13 St Helen's Place, London

After the passing of the Electricity (Supply) Act 1919, a scheme for supply in a largely extended area was put forward by the Company which formed the subject of an enquiry held at Llandudno in 1921 by the Electricity Commissioners and which resulted in the Order dated 3rd August 1923, constituting the North Wales and South Cheshire Electricity District and established the North Wales and South Cheshire Joint Electricity Authority. Certain powers, rights and obligations of the Joint Authority were transferred by deed to the Company, which then operated under the provisions contained in the Act of 1904, and the Order of 1923 throughout the extended area of supply covering 4080 square miles. The technical scheme put forward by the Company provided for the development of the water power resources of the district and the establishment of a new hydro-electric power station at Maentwrog with an installed capacity of not less than 15,000 kW.

Electricity became the prime focus of business for the Company, when in May 1923, a resolution was carried "that the name of the Company be changed from North Wales Power and Traction Company Ltd, to North Wales Power Company Ltd."

During this period, the rapidly increasing demands on the Power Company were met by the purchase of power in bulk from:

a) their associated company, The Aluminium Corporation Ltd, Dolgarrog.
b) The Mersey Power Company Ltd, Runcorn.

An interesting report relating to the then LNWR (London & North Western Railway) to be seen as reference D/KY/1279 in the Clwyd Record Office at Hawarden is reproduced in part here:

" Report to Sir Thomas Williams, by: F.A. Cortez-Leigh

Chief Electrical Engineers Office
Euston Station
NW1

June 11th 1920

Supply of electricity at Holyhead and Crewe

..............the situation at Holyhead where the present system is uneconomical, antiquated and inadequate..........

Two courses are open;

1. Erect outrown power station
2. The purchase of power in bulk

Objections to No.1 are the heavy capital expenditure; the rising price of coal and labour; the possibility of interruption to supply due to labour troubles.

The adoption of the second course would necessitate the provision of a transmission line to connect up the nearest power station of the North Wales Power Co. who it is stated will be the authorised undertakers for the North Wales District, in which Holyhead will be included under the new Electricity Supply Bill. The advantages would be:

a) the low working expenses of a water power station.
b) the water power costs are not affected by advances in wages to the same extent as steam power stations as there are less men employed in hydro-electric stations.
c) not affected by the rise in the price of coal.
d) not so subject to interruption as the station can be run by a few trained engineers who are not affected by trades disputes
e) plenty of scope for extension having regard to the large reserve of water power available

At Holyhead, the cost per unit from the railway's own power station and the corporation power station were in 1919 - 5.96 d(old pence) and 11.53d respectively.

By taking a supply in bulk from the North Wales power Company at $1^1/_4$d per unit there would be, it is estimated, a saving of £1,1000 per annum."

The LNWR obviously had a high regard for the Company's supply capabilities and lack of labour relations difficulties.

The Company constructed a double-circuit 33kV overhead transmission line between Percival Lane, Runcorn and their Crewe Substation in order to supply the requirements of the LNWR (later LMS) engineering works at Crewe until such time as the new hydro-electric works at Maentwrog became available (1928).

By a certificate dated 23rd October 1925, the Electricity Distribution of North Wales and District Ltd, was registered which operated eventually under numerous Electricity Orders ranging from the Pwllheli and Lleyn Order of 1926 to the Port Dinorwic Order of 1934 (totalling 18 Orders). The first appointed Directors were:

Henry Joseph Jack; Maenan Manor, Llanrwst[14]
Reginald Francis Legge; 10 Regents Park Road, London
George Victor Twiss; 22 St Johns Road, Golders Green, London
Arthur Francis Bott; The Lordship, Bennington, Stevenage

This company started construction in 1926 and completed the major proportion thereof in 1927. By the end of 1945, 51,214 consumers, representing a connected load of 89,500kW were connected. Supplies in all cases were derived from the transmission lines of the North Wales Power Co. at 6,600; 11,000 and 33,000 Volts. The non-statutory undertaking at Harlech was acquired in 1932 (this was the distribution system of the Aberartro scheme mentioned earlier in the text).

The Aluminium Corporation Ltd continued to supply power in bulk to the North Wales Power Co. until 1929, when as a result of the formation of the British Power and Light Corporation (1929) Ltd., the whole of the hydraulic works and the power stations at Dolgarrog were acquired by the Power Co. and were then operated in conjunction with the other power stations at Cwm Dyli and Maentwrog. The Power and Light Corp. gained controlling interests in the Power Co. holding over 99% of Share Capital and also acquired the whole of the issued Share Capital of the Electricity Distribution of North Wales and District Ltd.

In 1923 the total route length of transmission lines in operation by the NWPCo. was 110 miles. By 1937, the length in operation exceeded 900 route miles with an addition of 177 miles of secondary high pressure lines owned by their associated company, Electricity Distribution of North Wales and District Ltd, making a total of 1077 miles of transmission mains. In 1923, there were only 31 substations associated with the transmission system, but by 1937, the number, including pole-type substations was 570.

By the end of 1936, supply was being given at no less than 234 different points in the area, the connected load being approximately 43,500 kW and the number of consumers connected 34,665. The Local Authorities whom the Company supplied in bulk, themselves distributed to some 55,000 of their own consumers. The Company provided supply either directly or indirectly to some 100,000 consumers.

In 1939, the North Wales Power Co. acquired the undertaking of the Llanrwst Electricity Supply Co. Ltd; in 1937 the undertaking of the Llangefni Electric Light and Power Co. Ltd and in April 1939 the undertaking of the Betws-y-Coed Urban District Council.

For the year ended 31st December 1945, supply statistics were as follows:

Revenue sale of current	£1,470,582
Working Costs	£1,131,480
B.T.U. sold	374,363,138
Revenue per B.T.U. sold	0.94d
Costs per B.T.U. sold	0.72d

As a result of nationalisation, the North Wales Power Company Limited ceased to exist in vesting day in 1948.

Figures 14 & 15 follow - Original North Wales Power Company Ltd. advertisements reproduced by kind permission of Clwyd County Record Office.

Figure 14:

Domestic

NORTH WALES POWER COMPANY LTD.

SCALE OF CHARGES

(Anglesey, Bala and Dolwyddelen)

A—Flat Rate.

LIGHTING	**8d.** per unit.	Subject to a minimum charge of 7/6 for each Quarter.
HEATING ONLY ... (Where no Electric Cooking is installed)	**3d.** per unit for the first 50 units per quarter, and **1½d.** per unit for all units in excess of 50 per quarter.	
COOKING ONLY OR COOKING AND HEATING (Where both are installed)	**3d.** per unit for the first 50 units per quarter, and **1d.** per unit for all units in excess of 50 per quarter.	

B—Residential Tariff.

The Company is prepared to supply Electricity for LIGHTING and all other DOMESTIC PURPOSES at the low rate of 1½d. to 1d. per unit to consumers who agree to become yearly Subscribers to the Company's Service and pay the following subscription rate and unit charge:—

Subscription Rate.	**Unit Charge.**
4/- per assessable room per Quarter.	**1½d.** per unit for Lighting or Heating **reduced to** **1d.** per unit for all units in excess of Fifty per quarter if **ELECTRIC COOKING** is installed and used.

Assessable rooms include reception rooms, bedrooms, dressing rooms, billiards rooms, lounge halls, kitchens, and Farm Outbuildings. (Bathrooms, sculleries, passages, box-rooms, cellars, and garages, are not assessable).

The minimum number of assessable rooms shall be three, and the Company's decision on all matters appertaining to the classification of Rooms shall be final.

The Residential Tariff enables Subscribers to use Electricity for all purposes, including lighting, heating, and cooking at the same low price per unit. Under this system the more Electricity used the lower becomes the average price. Small appliances, such as electric irons, toasters, vacuum cleaners, etc., can be connected to the lamp holders or lighting plugs, whilst radiators and cooking appliances can be connected to the same meter, thus reducing installation costs and meter rents. Domestic power up to a maximum connected load of two horse-power can be used under the above tariff "B."

☞ *NOTE.*—**Reduced Price for Electric Cooking.** In order to qualify for a unit charge of 1d. per unit consumers must adopt electricity for their main Cooking requirements, and the Company reserves the right to require a minimum consumption of Electricity for that purpose.

QUARTERLY RENTALS FOR METERS, etc.

METERS:	For each 10 Amp Meter	**1/6**
	For each 20 Amp Meter	**2/0**
	For each 30 Amp Meter	**2/6**
	For each 40 Amp Meter	**3/0**
	For each 50 Amp Meter	**3/6**

Special Rates for Meters above 50 Amps.

TRANSFORMERS.—Where supply is given from extra high pressure lines a special Tariff is charged and a Rental is payable depending on size of Transformer, etc.

REF. 152/1/8828/5/34/5

SEE OVER

Figure 15:

CHARGES FOR SERVICE LINES

NOTE.—These Charges apply only to Service lines taken from existing Distributors passing the premises and available for General Supply.

OVERHEAD SERVICES (not exceeding 100 feet span of aerial cable).

FREE OF CHARGE up to 60 feet, including any portion of that amount which is on the Consumer's premises. All in excess of that length will be charged for at the rate of 9d. per foot (2-wire), and 1/6 per foot (4-wire).

UNDERGROUND SERVICES (not exceeding 100 feet route length).

FREE OF CHARGE up to a total of 60 feet, provided that the portion on Consumer's premises does not exceed 20 feet. All in excess of the above lengths respectively will be charged for at the rate of 2/- per foot (2-core), and 3/- per foot (4-core). Underground Service will only be given from an Overhead System subject to the consumer paying the full cost of this method.

NOTE.—All ordinary excavation and cutting away is included (except in the case of Buildings in the course of construction), **BUT NO POLES OR PERMANENT REINSTATEMENTS ON CONSUMER'S PREMISES.** *Special quotations will be made where poles are required and / or construction is of a special nature.*

GENERAL

Service Charges are payable in advance. The Company reserve the right to vary the scale of charges, on giving notice in writing to the Consumer.

The Company is *entitled*, by virtue of its statutory Powers, to charge for Electricity at the rate of 9d. per unit for Lighting, and 4d. per unit for Heating and Power when registered by a separate meter with a MINIMUM CHARGE, exclusive of meter rent, of 11/3 for ANY AMOUNT up to 15 units per Winter quarter, and 7/6 for ANY AMOUNT up to Ten units per Summer quarter.

The Flat Rate, however, has been reduced by the Company, see Rate A over page.

Further information and advice free of charge will be given on application to :

NORTH WALES POWER COMPANY LTD

North Wales Office: RHOSTYLLEN,
WREXHAM.
Telephone: Rhos 66
Telegrams: Aqualek, Wrexham.

or District Engineer.

ELECTRICITY HOUSE,
HIGH STREET,
JOHNSTOWN, NR. WREXHAM.
TEL. RHOS, 43

Chapter 5

PROPOSED SCHEMES

Apart from the hydro-electric plants of all categories that were constructed over a period of many years, several other schemes were proposed, surveys were undertaken and reports prepared. In a few instances, schemes came to fruition.

Documents in Public Records Office (PRO) classifications Power 2/28BOT; Power 2/36 and Power 14/255 give details of numerous proposals and reports and the following extracts summarise those details:

<u>Power 2/28 (BOT Committee Papers</u>[15]

Water Power Resources 1918 - Scottish and Welsh Water Powers.
Welsh Preliminary survey and report by Mr W Vaux Graham M.Inst.C.E.

1	*Scheme:*	*Llyn Can (Cader Idris)*
	Power House Location:	*On Afon Fawnog*
	Power developed estimate }: *available EHP at power house }*	*315*
	Total capital outlay:	*£21,380*
	Capital per EHP:	*£68*
2	*Scheme:*	*Trawsfynydd (Afon Prysor)*
	Power House Location:	*Junction of Afon Prysor and Afon Dwyryd*
	Power developed (EHP):	*4,425*
	Total capital outlay:	*£183,920*
	Capital per EHP:	*£42*

Note: this scheme was later developed by Maentwrog Power Station.

3	*Scheme:*	*Afon Rheidol (Devil's Bridge)*
	Power House Location:	*on river at Pontbren, Plwca*
	Power developed (EHP):	*6,500*
	Total capital outlay:	*£706,470*
	Capital per EHP:	*£109*
3a	*Scheme:*	*Afon Rheidol modified to supply industrial load for 10 hours per day. Bulk transmission of power to South Wales industrial area.*
	Power House Location:	*As in 3*
	Power developed (EHP):	*Maximum load, 15,600*
	Total capital outlay:	*£854,040*
	Capital per EHP:	*£55*

Estimated capital cost }
including transmission }: £1,002,390
lines and transformers }

Note: This scheme was to be developed by the Central Electricity Generating Board in the 1950's but is not within the scope of this work.

<u>Power 2/36</u>[16]
<u>Possible sources for the development of electricity from water power in Wales by Mr WJE Binnie 19:05:1919</u>

(Following instructions received from the Water Power Resources Committee, this report was prepared)

"......it must not be concluded that the table exhausts by any means the possibilities for the development of water power. There are many opportunities of utilising small quantities of power by means of comparatively inexpensive works......"

<u>Lake Bala</u> - this lake has been proposed as a possible source of water supply for London...... The objections to the development of this scheme are:

1. *the disturbance to the railway which skirts the bank on its Eastern side, which railway would have to be diverted if the lake level were raised to any material extent.*

2. *the flooding of the village of Bala (population 1537 in 1911).*

3. *the River Dee flows from the lake and the diversion of water would give rise to strenuous opposition.*

Note: It seems that Mr Binnie thought that a diversion of River Dee water would be strenuously opposed, whilst the possible flooding of Bala did not seem worthy of comment.

<u>Afon Tryweryn</u> - this scheme appears to represent opportunities of economical development......
Note: This scheme was eventually developed by Dwr Cymru/Welsh Water, refer to text on Llyn Celyn.
<u>Capel Curig</u> - ......we think that investigation would show that there are no difficulties regarding foundations and that the dimensions of the dam would be moderate......

The objection to this scheme would be chiefly based on sentimental grounds as there are falls on the river frequented by tourists (Swallow Falls)......as the existing main road through the valley would be submerged together with a large hotel, two small churches, a school and several other buildings.......

<u>Ogwen</u> - ...... storage can be economically obtained and a fall of about 290 feet can be secured in a distance of one quarter of a mile......

<u>Beddgelert</u> - this is an example of the development of a low fall - 180 feet; ample storage could be obtained by a dam of comparatively short length and the length of pressure tunnel would be 1¼ miles. The dam would be constructed above the village of Beddgelert...... there would be about 4 miles of road diversion.

In 1943, the North Wales power Company asked their consulting engineers for a report on the possibility of further hydro-electric development in North Wales. The report recommended the extension of the catchment areas of the existing stations at Dolgarrog and Maentwrog and the carrying out of 6 new projects. No action was taken before Vesting Date, but on 4th December 1948, the British Electricity Authority made the substance of the report public and implied that subject to further investigations and to consultation with all the interests affected, they proposed to adopt all the recommendations.

Power 14/255[17] reveals further information:

"...... original proposals were for schemes at:

1. *Conway (Penmachno)*
2. *Mawddach*
3. *Rheidol*
4. *Ffestiniog*
5. *Snowdon*
6. *Nant Ffrancon (Ogwen)*

The Government agreed that the BEA should proceed with the schemes at Maentwrog, Blaenau Ffestiniog and Dolgarrog, but no decision was made on the question of general powers (07.11.1951).

on 30th July 1951, BEA had formally applied for the Minister's consent under Section 10 of the Electricity Act 1947 to promote a Private Bill in Parliament for the schemes with the exception of those at Snowdon and Nant Ffrancon which they had decided to postpone.

The Minister of Local Government and Planning saw no objection to the extension of the catchment areas at Dolgarrog and Maentwrog, nor to the new stations(s) at Ffestiniog, but thought that the remaining three schemes at Conway, Mawddach and Rheidol should be rejected."

The schemes as proposed on 19th July 1951 had the following statistics:

Total installed capacity:	220 Megawatts
Energy in year of average rainfall:	402 million KWH
Estimated capital costs:	£22,878,000
Average total cost of energy:	0.65 pence per KWH

Opposition to the schemes appeared from several sources and included a letter from the National Parks Commission of 12th November 1951 to the Minister of Fuel and Power, signed by Sir Patrick Duff KCB, KCVO which stated *"......the four major schemes of Snowdon, Nant Ffrancon, Upper Conway and Mawddach would be so highly detrimental to the Park that we could not consistently with the responsibilities laid upon us by the National parks Act, do otherwise than resolutely oppose them."*

There was also a body known as the "North Wales (Hydro Electricity) Protection Committee". The Chairman was the Reverend HH Symonds and the Hon. Secretary, Mr TE Fairclough. The Committee's address for correspondence was 93a Scotland Road, Liverpool 3!!

The catchment extensions at Maentwrog and Dolgarrog were completed as described earlier. The hydro-electric scheme at Blaenau Ffestiniog was not proceeded with in its original form but a later scheme was completed which became the Ffestiniog pumped storage power station at Tanygrisiau.

Figure 16:

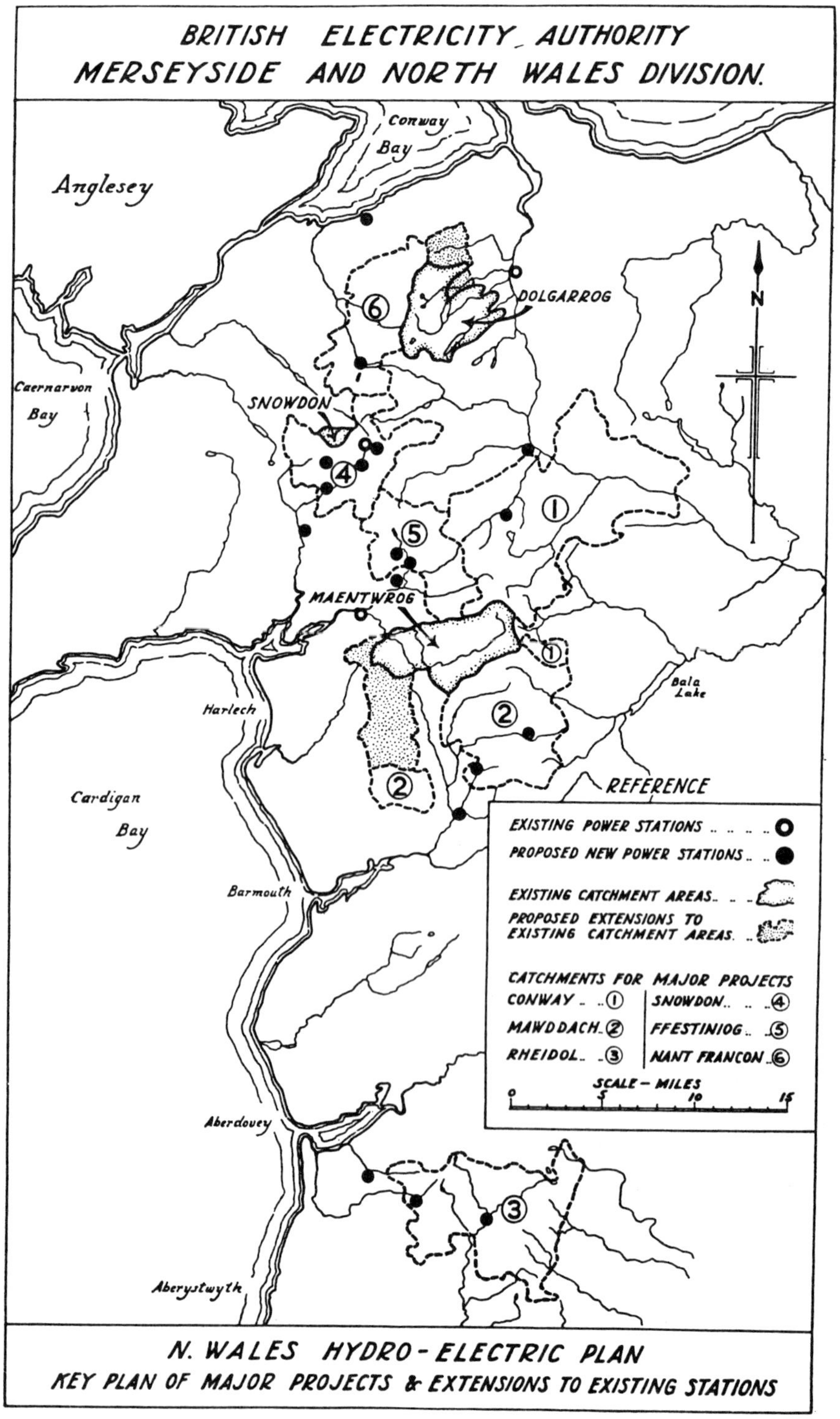

Chapter 6

ORGANISATION AND OPERATION

As previously mentioned, prior to 1948, the production, transmission and distribution of electricity was carried out by numerous undertakings of various sizes. Following the transfer of the industry into national ownership in that year, an attempt was made to retain all the best features of the old system, whilst introducing the benefits resulting from centralisation.

With effect from 1st April 1948, the power stations at Dolgarrog, Maentwrog, Cwm Dyli, Dolwen, Machynlleth, Dolgellau and Towyn became part of the British Electrical Authority (BEA). The letter initialed by H Gill sent to Maentwrog would have been repeated to other locations and is shown here for record purposes.

Figure 17: - Probably the last official communication on note paper headed "Electricity Distribution of North Wales and District Ltd." prior to nationalisation.

ELECTRICITY DISTRIBUTION OF NORTH WALES AND DISTRICT LTD.

To Station Superintendent,	*From* H. Gill.
Ref. Maentwrog.	*Ref.* Dolgarrog.

Form 24

30th March, 1948.

As you are aware the transfer of the ownership from the present undertaking to the British Electricity Authority takes effect on Thursday 1st April 1948. After then all Generation will come under Mr. A.R. Cooper, Divisional Controller for the Merseyside and North Wales Division with headquarters at:

British Electricity House,
Clarkes Gardens,
Woolton,
Liverpool.

The operation of the Power Stations and general procedure will continue as at present. To ensure the continued running of the plants on the same lines as before vesting date I have been appointed Senior Executive Officer and will no longer carry the designation Generation Engineer.

Arrangements have been made with the Area Board whereby the sending through of returns to Rhostyllen (Sub Area Office) will continue until affairs become organized at Divisional Headquarters and which will take time.

I am sending you 8 copies of a new magazine "Gridiron" price 4d. each. for disposal amongst members of your Staff. The Divisional Controller is responsible to a very large extent for its production and his aim is to publish matters of general interest to the personnel connected with Generating Stations etc., forming No.9 Division.

H.G.

With the passage of time came changes, the BEA was to become the Central Electricity Authority (CEA) which much later became the Central Electricity Generating Board (CEGB). The generation of electricity was controlled by the CEGB operating through its power stations in various generating regions. The CEGB also controlled the transmission of this electricity at high voltages to many supply points throughout England and Wales. At these points the distribution was taken over by the Area Electricity Boards, which for North Wales was the Merseyside and North Wales Electricity Board (MANWEB).

Resulting from the Electricity Act 1990, the remaining hydro-electric stations in public ownership, namely Cwm Dyli, Dolgarrog and Maentwrog, became part of the National Power Division of the CEGB as a prelude to full privatisation. For a short period these stations were then placed under the umbrella of National Power - Nuclear, but following the governmental decision that nuclear power stations would remain in public ownership, the hydro's with the exception of Maentwrog, were allotted to National Power plc. Maentwrog remained as part of the Nuclear Electric organisation due partly to the fact that the reservoir was shared with Trawsfynydd power station.

Cwm Dyli and Dolgarrog are presently part of National Power Hydro, whilst Maentwrog is operated by Magnox Electric, a division of Nuclear Electric plc.

In the era of the CEA and CEGB these stations were operated as part of the wider system and were controlled regarding generation instructions from Manchester (sometimes via Manweb's Legacy substation). Generation would take place according to reservoir storage levels; a merit order whereby the lowest cost power stations would provide base load, whilst the most expensive were called upon last; the system demand. The staff at the stations were limited to ensuring requested generation was achieved and could only assess their station's contribution by monitoring the system frequency.

Under the current regime, the stations operate in a completely commercial environment, the "big wheel" having turned back largely to the days of the old North Wales Power Company, whereby results are calculated on a financial basis. Because of their capacities, the stations are "non-centrally despatched" and are very much masters of their own destiny. Generation occurs at times of peak system prices, a different value appertaining to each half hour period for any day with the highest prices obviously relating to the periods of highest demand. Reservoir water storage management is of prime importance as is plant availability. Periods of generation are determined by station staff who will know beforehand the financial return to be obtained from the units generated and sold.

Chapter 7

PROSPECTS FOR THE FUTURE

The author remembers a period of "gloom and despondency" relating to the major hydro stations when decisions were made to spend as little money as possible in maintaining Cwm Dyli, and closure became a distinct possibility. The Dolgarrog site was earmarked for the construction of a gas turbine power station and when faults did occur on the hydro plant it was touch and go whether repairs were undertaken. It was a fact, of course, that the hydro stations were getting on in years but thankfully and sensibly, the necessary actions were taken which revitalised the situation.

As has already been stated in previous chapters, large capital investments have been made at Cwm Dyli, Dolgarrog and Maentwrog securing their future for at least another 60 years.

The chapter on "Proposed Schemes" contains a statement that "There are many opportunities of utilising small quantities of power by means of comparatively inexpensive works......". This statement is a relevant today as it was those many years ago, if not more so, because in the current financially dominant situation, for the hydro stations to stand still without progressing would inevitably have serious consequences.

Various schemes have been suggested, some have been subject to preliminary studies whilst others are at a more advanced stage. At the time of writing, National Power Hydro are pursuing two entirely contrasting schemes.

The first is a water treatment transfer scheme in conjunction with Dwr Cymru/Welsh Water, for the Dolgarrog catchment area. Substantial quantities of water from the Melynllyn/Dulyn reservoir previously used solely for water supply purposes will be diverted into the hydro station catchment via Llyn Eigiau and into Cowlyd reservoir. This extra water in Colwyd will enable Dwr Cymru to abstract additional water whilst also providing additional water for electricity generating. An added bonus for the hydro station will be the installation of a new small generator to take advantage of the diverted water flow.

The second scheme relates to a small plant at Cynwyd near Corwen, the existing reservoir having been previously used for hydro-electric purposes when owned by Colonel Vaughan Wynn. The local electricity board took the scheme over in 1949 and in about 1955 the Edeyrnion Rural District Council purchased the reservoir for water supply purposes and generation ceased. Dwr Cymru were the latest owners but the reservoir became surplus to their requirements and it is to be hoped that National Power will revive this site as a hydro-electric power station.

In recent times, conservation and renewable energy issues have become prominent, featuring regularly in media reports. As previously stated in the course of this work, hydro-electric schemes are not only environmentaly friendly but also employ a renewable source of energy. Due to these criteria there has been an awakenkng of interest in small hydro-electric schemes from companies who had previously not been interested in hydro-electric power, this is in marked contrast to the philosophy of some 20 years ago when "big is beautiful" seemed to be the key-phrase.

One such scheme which is currently operating successfully is located near to the village of Dolwyddelan (once in the county of Caernarvonshire). Designed and built for the Garnedd Power Company Limited, the scheme was conceived by the Company's principle Norman Weiss. The plant is remotely monitored and operated by Powergen from their Rheidol power station in mid-Wales.

The turbine house is situated in Blaenau Dolwyddelan where Blaenau means "upper" or "head of" in relation to the valley where the main river is the Lledr. The old established Garnedd farmhouse has a special significance in relation to non-conformism in North Wales, being the place where the celebrated preacher the Reverend John Jones "Talysarn" gave his first sermon. Across the valley floor close to the Roman Bridge railway station lies another old homestead, being Gorddinan, which gave its name to the pass over the mountain to Blaenau Ffestiniog before it became known in more recent times as the Crimea pass. Although historically significant, the area witnessed the early presence of electricity in the form of overhead transmission lines from the power station at Cwm Dyli which climbed over the "Cribau" on their way to the Oakeley quarries. Close by was a site investigated by the CEGB as a possible location for a pumped storage scheme prior to the construction of the existing Dinorwic project. The old North Wales Power Company licated a transmission depot in Roman Bridge and the old pioneers would be delighted to know that an unobtrusive scheme is currently utilising the natural resources in this historic location.

The Garnedd is a "run-off" river scheme utilising and exploiting the waters of "Ceunant Ty'n-y-ddol" a tributary of the Lledr. Water from the river is diverted via a small head pond into a 600mm buiried pipeline which is 1km long. The static head is 102 metres. The turbine house was relocated 50m upstream from its originally planned location in order to avoid a site of archaeological importance. An agreed flow is maintained in the river at all times and the discharged water having passed through the turbine, flows into the river.

The turbine house contains a Turgo impulse twin jet turbine manufactured by Gilbert Gilkes and Gordon Limited, an organisation which has featured prominently throughout this history. The turbine drives a synchronous generator of 600kW maximum output and average annual generation is 2.3Gwh. All the control equipment is also housed in this stone clad building.

Tha main contract was placed in July 1991 and initial generation commenced in February 1992. Capital cost of the scheme amounted to £700,000.

The future prospects are therefore promising - long live hydro!

Photo 69: The Author seated at the communications desk in the control room of Ffestiniog pumped storage power station in 1961.

BIBLIOGRAPHY & REFERENCES

1 Dorothy Sylvester; A History of Gwynedd; Philimore & Co. Ltd.

2 Emrys Hughes & Aled Eames: Porthmadog Ships; Gwynedd Archives Service

3 Public Record Office, Chancery Lane, London

4 Public Record Office, Chancery Lane, London

5 Public Record Office, Ruskin Avenue, Kew

6 Gwynedd Archives Service, Dolgellau

7 Public Record Office, Chancery Lane, London

8 JG Isherwood; Slate from Blaenau Ffestiniog; AB Publishing

9 Alan Holmes; Slate from Abergynolwyn; Gwynedd Archives

10 Gwynedd Archives Service, Dolgellau

11 Gwynedd Archives Service, Dolgellau

12 Public Record Office, Chancery Lane, London

13 David Bick; The Old Copper Mines of Snowdonia

14 Eric Jones & David Gwyn; Dolgarrog an Industrial History; Gwynedd Archives - contains interesting detail regarding Henry J Jack as well as further information relating to Dolgarrog

15 Public Record Office, Ruskin Avenue, Kew

16 Public Record Office, Ruskin Avenue, Kew

17 Public Record Office, Ruskin Avenue, Kew